THE 12 STEPS
A WAY OUT

*A Working Guide for Adult Children
from Addictive and Other Dysfunctional Families*

Friends in Recovery

Recovery Publications, Inc.
1201 Knoxville Street
San Diego, CA 92110
(619) 275-1350

Published by Recovery Publications, Inc.
1201 Knoxville Street
San Diego, CA 92110
(619) 275-1350

The Twelve Steps have been reprinted and adapted with permission from Alcoholics Anonymous World Services, Inc. The opinions expressed are not to be attributed to Alcoholics Anonymous, nor does *The 12 Steps—A Way Out* imply any endorsement by AA.

Printed in the United States of America

Second Printing April 1987
Third Printing July 1987
Fourth Printing October 1987
Fifth Priting August 1988
Sixth Printing January 1989 Revised Edition
Seventh Printing June 1989

Recovery Publications, Inc.

The 12 Steps—A Way Out: A Working Guide for Adult Children from Addictive and Other Dysfunctional Families.

1.   2.   1.Title
ISBN 0-9414105-07-9 pbk $14.95.

*In memory of Edward, Cecilia and the countless others
whose lives were a struggle with addiction,
and who never found "a way out."*

*This book is especially dedicated to those family members
and friends who have found the courage to seek recovery.*

*In appreciation of the many Adult Children who participated in the
experimental Step Study Writing Workshops. Their courage and willingness
to participate and provide feedback was a vital contribution to this book.*

TABLE OF CONTENTS

THE TWELVE STEPS OF ALCOHOLICS ANONYMOUS

1. We admitted we were powerless over alcohol—that our lives had become unmanageable.

2. Came to believe that a Power greater than ourselves could restore us to sanity.

3. Made a decision to turn our will and our lives over to the care of God as we understood Him.

4. Made a searching and fearless moral inventory of ourselves.

5. Admitted to God, to ourselves, and to another human being the exact nature of our wrongs.

6. Were entirely ready to have God remove all these defects of character.

7. Humbly asked Him to remove our shortcomings.

8. Made a list of all persons we had harmed, and became willing to make amends to them all.

9. Made direct amends to such people wherever possible, except when to do so would injure them or others.

10. Continued to take personal inventory and when we were wrong promptly admitted it.

11. Sought through prayer and meditation to improve our conscious contact with God as we understood Him, praying only for knowledge of His will for us and the power to carry that out.

12. Having had a spiritual awakening as the result of these steps, we tried to carry this message to alcoholics, and to practice these principles in all our affairs.

Reprinted with permission of
ALCOHOLICS ANONYMOUS WORLD SERVICES, INC.

INTRODUCTION TO REVISED EDITION

This material was first written in 1986 exclusively for Adult Children who were working the Twelve Steps in a supportive environment. Since the first publication in 1987, the book has been reprinted six times. With each printing, text changes were made which clarified and amplified the message. The writing exercises and group techniques have also been improved and expanded as a result of feedback from group participants.

The Twelve Step program enables us to share our experience, strength and hope with others. Many newcomers to the Program can relate to the Common Feelings and Behaviors but have difficulty in identifying alcoholism in their family. Many recovering professionals and individuals who are studying alcoholism and other addictions have contributed largely to the development of new insights and material relating to these issues. Their studies and experiences indicate that addictive behavior is an obsessive-compulsive disorder. It represents an obsession or craving which drives a person to compulsive use of relationships, alcohol, food, drugs, sex, gambling, etc. in order to fill an inner void or emptiness. This contribution has expanded the understanding of the term "addiction" and has been beneficial to the revision of this book.

This revised edition reflects the spiritual and emotional growth of its contributors, who continue to work their individual programs and apply the principles of the Twelve Steps to their daily lives. Each of them has found the root of their recovery process to be their partnership with a Higher Power. Since individual understanding of a Higher Power varies, the use of the male pronoun to describe that Power has been deleted.

As part of the revision of this book, the wording in Steps One, Two, Six and Seven have been altered. The changes are summarized as follows.

Step One, now states that we are powerless over the effects of addiction, rather than alcohol. As research continues in the field of addiction, it is becoming evident that we are an addictive society—with addiction being so pervasive that we cannot identify all its manifestations.

Step Two has been changed to read "restored to wholeness." The philosophy of the Twelve Steps views partnership with our Higher Power as the foundation for achieving wholeness. This book is intended to help us explore our childhood family systems to discover the ways in which our wholeness was violated and our true selves gradually distorted.

Steps Six and Seven focus on working in partnership with our Higher Power in order to continue moving away from our past and toward healing and wholeness. Belief in a Higher Power does not entitle us to any magical cure or sudden relief from pain. We come to realize that the thoughts, feelings and inner urges to return to our old behaviors require our conscious effort not to repeat them again. We can gradually accomplish this task of "letting go" by asking for and depending on the love, acceptance and strength of our Higher Power. It's called Team Work.

We walked away from our dysfunctional homes and childhoods with distorted views and beliefs about ourselves and the world. Having seen ourselves reflected in our parental mirrors, we adopted beliefs that we were "not okay." In doing so, we gave up our identity and began searching for ways to feel good about ourselves. As adults, we continue this pattern by allowing others to influence our self-image, self-esteem and happiness. Our self-defeating beliefs about ourselves lead us to make self-destructive choices. Thus, we end up seeking to fill our inner emptiness with inappropriate behavior and misuse of other people, sex, chemicals, possessions, accomplishment, money, etc.

As we begin our recovery, changes in our feelings and behavior may mean we "act as if" things have changed. This "act of faith" helps us in our process toward "coming to believe" that there is a Power greater than ourselves who is there for us. This Power may be primarily a belief in our Inner Self, God, Life, etc. and only secondarily based upon an intellectual conviction. We may be comfortable thinking of our new belief as more like falling in love than adopting a philosophy.

Our journey toward wholeness is clearly one that will last for the rest of our lives. The "leap of faith" we take is not the admission that "I believe," for we can only truly believe that for which we have found sufficient evidence. It is an act of courage and risk-taking. Our first steps of faith will undoubtedly constitute looking for evidence, and the greatest evidence of all will be our firsthand experience with our Higher Power.

We take the existence and availability of the incandescent bulb for granted, but it was the faith of Thomas Edison, plus years of trial and error, that led to that discovery. Knowing that it may take us weeks, months and perhaps years to find and learn to work with our Higher Power, should we not begin? By facing the challenge presented in this book, we will be putting forth the same dedication and curiosity as Edison—sitting down before the facts as we know them, prepared to relinquish our preconceived notions.

Remembering the wisdom of the Chinese proverb about the journey of a thousand miles starting with the first step, we need only begin.

THE TWELVE STEPS AND
OUR JOURNEY TOWARD WHOLENESS

The Twelve Step program is a philosophy of life which helps us to recognize the benefits of discovering and expanding our spiritual nature. It is not a program sponsored by any particular religious group or entity. Though people using this program find it harmonious with their own personal theology and spiritual beliefs, it has no official religious affiliation. It is a program we follow at our own pace and in our own way, utilizing the help and support of our Higher Power and others who also work the Program.

This book illustrates how the Twelve Steps can be used as an initial recovery tool and later integrated into an ongoing part of our journey toward wholeness. As we begin to recognize and work on our life problems in the light of the Twelve Steps, we develop the foundation for a recovery experience that can bring about our physical, emotional, mental and spiritual well-being. An open mind and a willingness to do the work are all that is required.

The material in this book focuses on the individual, but is also being used successfully in groups as a Step Study Writing Workshop. The format used in these workshops includes the formation of small "family groups" that work independently for a portion of the meeting, and then gather together as one group during the final segment for general sharing. The workshops are not intended to be a substitute for professional therapy. They are opportunities for increasing our self-awareness in the supportive, caring fellowship of people in recovery.

The workshops can be the source of many personal benefits and rewards. In the small family groups, healthy communication skills can be learned, trust can develop, secrets and feelings can be disclosed and the process of healing and loving self-parenting can begin. Workshop participation is a step toward breaking out of the isolation and alienation we experience as Adult Children. Our loneliness will lessen as friendships with other group members develop. We can experience being close to others by giving as well as receiving supportive and thoughtful feedback. Communication outside of the meetings is a vital element in the workshop process. In order to keep the feeling of "family" alive, participants are encouraged to call one another by phone as well as to socialize outside of the regular meeting times.

The format of the Twelve Step material in this book is only one of the many creative tools available to individuals on the path toward recovery. It provides a guideline to help us achieve our goals of peace and serenity. As our relationship with a Higher Power develops, more will be disclosed to us and our lives will become less complicated. We learn to ask our Higher Power for help in understanding what we can do to take better care of ourselves. By working the Steps, greater and deeper insights will occur.

Willingness to complete this material and a commitment to work the Steps on a daily basis will provide us with the ongoing gifts of peace and serenity. As we share our experience, strength and hope we join our fellows on the journey to wholeness and are unified in the Fellowship of the Spirit.

INTRODUCTION

As Adult Children from addictive or other dysfunctional families, we have had to face many difficulties in our lives. The attitudes, feelings and behaviors we have today are the direct result of the modeling and messages we experienced in our early environment. Because we grew up in chaos, we did not learn appropriate interpersonal or decision-making skills, or the value of recognizing cause and effect—that every behavior brings with it a consequence.

We continue to resist recognizing these limitations in ourselves. This may cause us to suffer from maladjustment and experience severe psychological, emotional and behavioral stress. Our denial is the key to that resistance. It is our defense against the reality of our condition and keeps us unaware of our compulsive or obsessive behaviors. These behaviors manifest themselves through various means, some of which are; need to be in control, lack of self-confidence or personal esteem, being victims or martyrs, an inability to express our needs and feelings and being unaware of our repressed feelings of pain, resentment, shame, fear and rage.

When a life circumstance forces us to come to terms with ourselves, we start looking for explanations. We try self-help books, therapy groups and other forms of consciousness raising. After exhausting these resources, we come to the realization that the peace we seek is not to be found in these sources. When we reach this point, we are ready to accept the support and guidance of a Higher Power. Our acceptance and reliance upon this spiritual partner is brought to fruition as we work the Twelve Steps and receive the budding miracle of our faith and efforts—the restoration of our trust, dignity, courage and newness of life.

THE TWELVE STEPS FOR ADULT CHILDREN

STEP ONE
We admitted we were powerless over the effects of addiction—that our lives had become unmanageable.

STEP TWO
Came to believe that a Power greater than ourselves could restore us to wholeness.

STEP THREE
Made a decision to turn our will and our lives over to the care of God as we understood God.

STEP FOUR
Made a searching and fearless moral inventory of ourselves.

STEP FIVE
Admitted to God, to ourselves, and to another human being the exact nature of our wrongs.

STEP SIX
Were entirely ready to work in partnership with God to remove our ineffective behavior.

STEP SEVEN
Humbly asked God to help us remove our shortcomings.

STEP EIGHT
Made a list of all persons we had harmed and became willing to make amends to them all.

STEP NINE
Made direct amends to such people wherever possible, except when to do so would injure them or others.

STEP TEN
Continued to take personal inventory and, when we were wrong, promptly admitted it.

STEP ELEVEN
Sought through prayer and meditation to improve our conscious contact with God as we understood God, praying only for knowledge of God's will for us and for the power to carry that out.

STEP TWELVE
Having had a spiritual awakening as the result of these steps, we tried to carry this message to others, and to practice these principles in all our affairs.

PREPARATORY INFORMATION
FOR STEP STUDY GROUPS

Appendix One contains suggested methods of study for people participating in a Step Study Writing Workshop. The recommendations are based upon the personal experiences of many people who have used the materials. This section provides specific guidelines for starting and conducting a Step Study Writing Workshop.

Appendix Two includes sample meeting designs and useful suggestions for conducting the Step Study Writing Workshop.

In Appendix Three, there are weekly exercises to be used during each meeting. These exercises are valuable tools for groups discussing the materials relative to the Step being studied.

NOTICE

This book is designed to provide information regarding the subject matter covered. It is provided with the understanding that the publisher and author are not engaged in rendering individualized professional services. These processes and questions, intended for individual or group study, are not to be a substitute for one-to-one professional therapy when such help is necessary.

NOTE FROM THE PUBLISHER

Those who participated in the writing and review of this material are recovering Adult Children from dysfunctional families. Their intention was to carry the message of the Twelve Steps to all individuals who experienced trauma in their childhood. Central to the theme of this work is that healing is possible for those individuals whose childhood has been impacted by addictive or emotionally repressive parents or guardians. The insight they brought to the writing of this book was a result of their belief that, through working the Twelve Steps and developing a loving supportive partnership with one's Higher Power, one could be restored to wholeness.

Their intention is to offer a workable tool for writing one's own personal story of recovery. This has been achieved by presenting the conditions most commonly found in Adult Children in tandem with the Twelve Steps as adapted from Alcoholics Anonymous. The philosophical foundation for this book is based upon the Twelve Step concept that has helped millions of individuals recover from many forms of addictive, compulsive or obsessive behavior. The material emphasizes the application of one's self-understanding and awareness as a major recovery tool.

The Twelve Traditions of Alcoholics Anonymous stress personal anonymity as a vital element in one's recovery. "Friends in Recovery" have chosen to remain anonymous for that reason. We offer these materials, not as an end in themselves, but as a means to developing a healthy relationship with God and with others.

COMMON FEELINGS AND BEHAVIORS
OF ADULT CHILDREN

Research involving individuals who were raised in an addictive or dysfunctional family environment has determined that certain feelings and behaviors are common in Adult Children from these homes. Although the general population demonstrates many of these behaviors, individuals from dysfunctional families tend to have a high incidence of them. This exercise is intended to help identify the areas of your life in which these feelings and behaviors are evident.

We have feelings of low self-esteem as a result of being criticized. We perpetuate these parental messages by judging ourselves and others harshly. We try to cover up our poor opinions of ourselves by being perfectionistic, controlling, contemptuous and gossipy.

- In what ways do you think, feel or act in an effort to compensate for your feelings of low self-esteem? _____

_____

_____

_____

We tend to isolate ourselves out of fear and to feel uneasy around other people, especially authority figures.

- Give examples of how you isolate yourself from other people. _____

_____

_____

_____

- What difficulty do you have dealing with people in authority? _____

_____

_____

_____

We are desperate for love and approval and will do anything to make people like us. Not wanting to hurt others, we remain "loyal" in situations and relationships even when evidence indicates our loyalty is undeserved.

- In what ways do you seek approval from your family or friends? _____

_____

_____

_____

- Cite an example where your extreme loyalty is undeserved. _____
_____
_____
_____

We are intimidated by angry people and personal criticism. This causes us to feel inadequate and insecure.

- What is your first recollection of being intimidated by an angry person? _____
_____
_____
_____

- How do you respond to personal criticism? _____
_____
_____
_____

We continue to attract emotionally unavailable people with addictive personalities.

- Describe your relationships involving people with addictive/compulsive personality styles (e.g. alcoholic, workaholic, gambler, overeater, religious fanatic). _____
_____
_____
_____

- Describe the relationships from which you receive nurturing and support. _____
_____
_____
_____

We live life as victims, blaming others for our circumstances, and are attracted to other victims as friends and lovers. We confuse love with pity and tend to "love" people we can pity and rescue.

- Describe an instance in which you were drawn into a situation or relationship where you were victimized. _____
_____
_____
_____

- List things you do for others that indicate you are trying to rescue them. _____

_____

_____

_____

We are either super-responsible or super-irresponsible. We take responsibility for solving others' problems or expect others to be responsible for solving ours.. This enables us to avoid being responsible for our own lives and choices.

- Describe those areas of your life in which you feel either super-responsible or super-irresponsible. _____

_____

_____

_____

We feel guilty when we stand up for ourselves or act in our own best interest. We give in to others' needs and opinions instead of taking care of ourselves.

- Identify recent situations in which you were afraid to express your desires or feelings and, instead, gave in to others. _____

_____

_____

_____

We deny, minimize or repress our feelings as a result of our traumatic childhoods. We are unaware of the impact that our inability to identify and express our feelings has had on our adult lives.

- How do you express your feelings and acknowledge them when something is upsetting you in your work or relationships? _____

_____

_____

_____

We are dependent personalities who are so terrified of rejection or abandonment that we tend to stay in situations or relationships that are harmful to us. Our fears and dependency stop us from ending unfulfilling relationships and prevent us from entering into fulfilling ones.

- In which of your present relationships do you fear rejection or abandonment? _____

_____

_____

_____

- How do you deal with this fear? _____
  _____
  _____
  _____

Denial, isolation, control, shame and inappropriate guilt are legacies from our family of origin. As a result of these symptoms, we feel hopeless and helpless.

- Having been a victim of family dysfunction, describe which symptoms are most prevalent? _____
  _____
  _____
  _____

We have difficulty with intimacy, security, trust and commitment in our relationships. Lacking clearly defined personal limits and boundaries, we become enmeshed in our partner's needs and emotions.

- Describe your present difficulties with intimate relationships. _____
  _____
  _____
  _____

We tend to procrastinate and have difficulty following projects through from beginning to end.

- Describe projects you have started and have not completed from lack of motivation or procrastination. _____
  _____
  _____
  _____

We have a strong need to be in control. We overreact to change over which we have no control.

- What do you fear most when you are not in control? _____
  _____
  _____
  _____

STEP ONE

We admitted we were powerless over the effects of addiction —
that our lives had become unmanageable.

❧

The idea presented in Step One is overwhelming to most of us until we begin to accept the reality of our lives as they actually are. It is humiliating to admit that we are powerless and that our lives have become unmanageable. We have spent a major portion of our lives attempting to manage the behavior, thoughts and feelings of others so that we could feel safe and secure. Some of us may strive for control by appearing weak and incapable, thereby manipulating others to perform for us. We may be obsessed with achieving a superior status in life, and we find it difficult to acknowledge that we could actually be powerless. We may be preoccupied with being the smartest or the fastest, or with having the best job. Whatever we do, no matter how hard we try to make it appear okay, some of our behavior puts our health and well-being at serious risk. Step One brings us to the threshold of identifying the causes of the obsessive and compulsive behavior that we cannot control.

- List examples of your attempts to manipulate the thoughts, feelings and behaviors of others. _____

  _____

  _____

  _____

- Describe some of your behaviors that are damaging to your health and well-being. _____

  _____

  _____

  _____

We realize that, in this life, we have the power to make choices about matters which affect us. In attempting to influence and manage the outcome of those choices, we may sometimes experience conflict. Prior to becoming aware of our problem, we sense that something is wrong and that life is unfulfilling in many ways. As a natural result, we desperately try to right the wrong by "fixing" things. No matter what we do or where we turn, we continue to suffer acute anxiety attacks or experience episodes of bizarre and compulsive behavior. When we finally are forced to look closely at ourselves and see that we have exhausted all other possibilities, we are ready for Step One. At this point, we have no alternative but to admit that we are powerless and that our lives have become unmanageable. For the first time, we begin to alter the course of our lives, and strive for healing.

- How does it feel to think of yourself as being powerless? _____
  _____
  _____
  _____

- Which events caused you to become concerned about the unmanageability of your life?
  _____
  _____
  _____

Step One is the foundation for all the Steps. When working this Step, we begin to acknowledge the reality of our life experiences. It is important not to judge ourselves harshly—we need only to observe our behavior and admit that we are powerless to change it. As we surrender to this idea, we see our behavior, thoughts and feelings as they really are and recognize the need for greater honesty with ourselves and others. It is through confronting and admitting our powerlessness that we begin to risk being honest about our limitations.

- Describe your behaviors and attitudes that indicate you are operating in a less-than-honest manner and need help. _____
  _____
  _____
  _____

Step One consists of two distinct parts: (1) admitting that we are powerless over the affects of addictive or dysfunctional behavior from our childhood caregivers, and (2) admitting that our lives have been, and will continue to be, unmanageable if we do not change.

- Give examples of being powerless and describe your feelings that result from being powerless. _____
  _____
  _____
  _____

- Give examples of where your life is unmanageable and describe your feelings about it.
  _____
  _____
  _____

Admitting our powerlessness over the affects of addictive or dysfunctional behavior from our childhood caregivers often is the catalyst that brings us to the Program. Through the Program, we initiate a process of recovery that can transform our lives. Our ineffective behavior has not supported our well-being, and our often self-destructive lifestyle is a major factor contributing to our condition. We now understand how we obtained our distorted life-view of the world, ourselves and others. This view has been perpetuated through our acquired traits, habits and behaviors. Recalling our childhood, we realize that, years before we recognized it, we behaved ineffectively and were out of control. Even then, our obsessions were not simply habits, but, indeed, the beginning of a progressive behavioral disorder involving our mental, physical and emotional well-being.

● What memories illustrate most vividly your unhealthy childhood environment? _____

_____

_____

_____

● Describe the feelings that accompany those memories (e.g., anger, sadness, fear). _____

_____

_____

_____

Our minds cry out against the idea of personal powerlessness and resist acknowledging that, in reality, we are not in charge. We are accustomed to accepting full responsibility for the events in our lives, as well as in the lives of others. This supports our need to deny that we are powerless. Until we discover how we can be responsible persons and also be powerless, we cannot take the first step toward liberating ourselves from the bondage of our past. The degree to which we are able to surrender is the degree to which we acknowledge our powerlessness.

● List the things for which you believe you are responsible. _____

_____

_____

_____

● How has accepting responsibility for the lives of others affected your ability to function?

_____

_____

_____

Admitting that our lives are unmanageable is as compromising to our self-image as admitting that we are powerless. We want to see ourselves as responsible adults—holding a job, managing a house and family and functioning normally. We have been taught from childhood that the only way to be successful is to be in control. We have received repeatedly the message that successful people manage their own lives, as well as the lives of others, without needing outside help.

● In what ways do you feel overwhelmed or stressed by all that you are concerned about? __

_____

_____

_____

- List five areas of your life that are unmanageable. Which one is the most unmanageable?

  _____

  _____

  _____

When we accept the fact that our lives are unmanageable, we also will recognize that ultimate control of our lives is not in our hands. As we reflect on the condition of our lives, we can see that, no matter how we exerted control, the results were never quite what we planned. Realizing that our depressions and frustrations are signs that we are not as competent as we think, we become more realistic in identifying the extent of our unmanageability. We see how we rationalize our behavior by making excuses for ourselves and blaming our action or inaction on fatigue, stress or other people. As we examine our lives more objectively, including our part in what is wrong with our lives, we drop our disguises and become more honest with ourselves. We then see that our lives are clearly unmanageable and not at all what we would like them to be.

- Describe a situation in which someone you trust expressed concern about your behavior.

  _____

  _____

  _____

- Who expressed concern and how did you feel at the time? _____

  _____

  _____

  _____

Though the first Step may seem overwhelming, it merely indicates and emphasizes our human limitations, which have been a source of discomfort to us for a long time. For most of our lives, we have tried to hide our imperfections from ourselves and others, thus avoiding the reality of our situation. Step One is the first step toward developing the humility we need to accept and rely on spiritual guidance from a Higher Power. This simple act opens the door to the healing change we seek.

- List the major self-limitations that have caused you intense discomfort. _____

  _____

  _____

  _____

- What are your feelings about each of these limitations? _____

  _____

  _____

  _____

In the process of accepting our powerlessness and acknowledging the unmanageability of our lives, we see that our attempts to hide our limitations have crippled us. Although working Step One can be painful, the road to recovery can only begin with honest self-confrontation and surrender. Until we do this, our progress toward recovery will be hindered. Although it is difficult for many of us to accept our present condition, we realize that we alone cannot manage our own lives or control our thinking. Admitting our human limitations forms the foundation for working each of the Twelve Steps.

- List the behaviors you need to change so you can experience healing (e.g., relationship addiction, always having to be right, overpowering guilt, non-assertiveness, fear of abandonment). _____

  _____

  _____

  _____

- What consequences resulted from each of these behaviors (e.g., violence, unhappiness, feeling out of control, fear of intimacy)? _____

  _____

  _____

  _____

- What do you say or think to yourself (self-talk) that prompts the above behavior (e.g., *"He is not going to do this to me again!"*)? _____

  _____

  _____

  _____

- What is your life-rule that prompts self-talk and the subsequent behaviors (e.g., *"When I grow up, no one is going to push me around." "If I don't get them first, they will take advantage of me."*)? _____

  _____

  _____

  _____

Notes: _____

STEP TWO

Came to believe that a power greater than ourselves
could restore us to wholeness.

❧

Accepting our powerlessness leads us naturally into Step Two. By this time, we have discovered the impact that being raised in a dysfunctional family has had on our lives. Our present condition is a result of the many decisions we made to survive in that chaotic environment. We are now faced with behavior that produces unmanageable situations over which we are powerless. For some of us, belief in the strength of our self-will was all we thought we needed until, in Step One, we realized the true state of our ineffective behavior. As we accept the idea of a Power greater than ourselves, we begin to function in a healthier way, and our lives become more manageable. We recognize that we are just human beings, learning to live within our human limitations.

● Describe the fears that block your acceptance of a Higher Power? _____

_____

_____

_____

Step Two is referred to as the Hope Step. It is the starting point from which we begin our journey toward a more spiritual view of life. In Step One, when we recognized our condition, we felt hopeless and beaten. Step Two instills new hope, as we see that help is available if we simply take the risk to believe and trust in a Power greater than ourselves. If we follow the guidance of that Power, we no longer need to struggle. We now have a chance to dramatically decrease our old patterns of behavior and gradually become the persons we were meant to be. Step Two provides a foundation for the spiritual development that will help us achieve a greater sense of personal fulfillment.

● What is your understanding of a Higher Power at this point? Describe the attributes of

that Power. _____

_____

_____

_____

● The Twelve Steps have a spiritual foundation. What does this mean to you? _____

_____

_____

_____

As newcomers, we often encounter stumbling blocks when working this Step. One obstacle is the difficulty we have in believing that a Power greater than ourselves exists. Although we may be aware of many examples in which "faith as small as a mustard seed" has worked wonders in the lives of others, we may doubt that it could apply to us. If doubt persists, we could be resisting the idea of a Higher Power's healing presence. We may find it impossible to imagine that, through "believing," the intensity of our obsessions and compulsions could decrease. In time, our faith begins to grow as we recognize that even the most devout, spiritually grounded persons suffer moments of doubt.

- What does "faith as small as a mustard seed" mean to you? _____

_____

_____

_____

Another problem posed by Step Two is the implication that disorder and ineffective behavior permeates our lives. Having recognized that our lives are unmanageable, we now know that we need new direction. These are powerful issues for us; they can be frightening when we face them for the first time. For many of us, they are definite contradictions of our former beliefs about ourselves and our lives.

- What do you hope to gain by accepting the concept of a Higher Power? _____

_____

_____

_____

Before entering the Program, many of us strongly resisted spiritual concepts and beliefs. We neither understood spirituality, nor felt it had anything to offer us. Our longing for the nurturing and caring parent, absent from our childhood, limited our ability to understand the concept of a trusting and loving Higher Power. Perhaps we felt that our prayers were unanswered. Our faith in a Higher Power may have been shattered by our belief that, if God exists, it is not a loving God. Often, our low self-esteem created the feeling that we were not worthy of the attention or care of a Higher Power, or that it could even exist.

- List experiences that caused you to distrust the idea of a Power greater than yourself.

_____

_____

_____

- What do you remember about the spiritual environment in your home? How do these memories influence your feelings today? _____

_____

_____

_____

In Step One, we established a foundation for accepting the existence of a Higher Power. Having admitted our powerlessness, we realize how self-will has impacted our lives. The discovery and acceptance of a Power greater than ourselves is the beginning of our turning away from our self-will. Through working the Steps, we can experience a growing trust in our Higher Power.

- How has your self-will controlled your life and dominated your actions? _____
_____
_____
_____

- How does the phrase "self-will run riot" apply to you? _____
_____
_____
_____

Many people have found that "coming to believe" is a natural result of attending meetings on a regular basis. Through working the Program, it becomes evident that something dynamic is happening. If we are willing to keep an open mind and recognize the success that others enjoy, we can expect that, in time, it will also happen for us.

- What is your pattern of attending meetings? _____
_____
_____
_____

- How do you see attendance at meetings as necessary to your effectively working the Program? _____
_____
_____
_____

When we encounter our ineffective behavior and can surrender to the Twelve Step process, the existence of a Higher Power becomes very real to us. We shift our attention from wanting to alter our behavior to understanding that life is a process of evolutionary change. This shift of focus attests to the presence of a Higher Power—assisting, empowering and enabling us to accomplish what we could not have accomplished under our own power.

- List examples of your willingness to trust in the promises of the Program and to accept the idea of a Higher Power being available to you. _____
_____
_____
_____

During the initial stages of accepting the presence of a Higher Power, it is sometimes helpful to be consciously aware of the special occurrences around us. We can view coincidences in our lives as small miracles, gifts or simply interventions of our Higher Power. By taking the time to thank our Higher Power for simple things like "not getting a ticket for running a red light," or "receiving an unexpected call from someone we are thinking about," we learn to accept a Higher Power. Our willingness to express gratitude to this Power assists us as we "come to believe."

● Cite examples of events or experiences in your life that demonstrate your awareness of a Higher Power? _____

_____

_____

_____

Step Two does not demand that we accept the definitions of God as presented by various religious organizations or specific denominations. In fact, our belief may come from simply experiencing the strength of our Higher Power's healing at work in our lives. More and more we recognize the genius of our Higher Power in the loving kindness of a friend, the loyalty of a partner, the comfort and help we receive from a person in the Program, or even the Program itself.

● Explain the God of your understanding. How do you interact with that God? _____

_____

_____

_____

Belief in a Power greater than ourselves is central to becoming the happy, positive and loving persons we are truly meant to be. Our old self-centered way has possibly led us to the depths of despair and loneliness, causing us to become detached from ourselves and others. We discover that our analytical mind, with its fears, judgments, expectations and plans, cannot solve our problems. The more we try to resolve things by ourselves, or expect someone else to resolve them, the more difficult our lives become.

● Why is belief in a Higher Power central to your being able to lead a fully rewarding life?

_____

_____

_____

Step Two helps us see that our lives can be restored to wholeness. In the context of the Program, wholeness is defined as "being in sound health, not diseased or injured, not broken, damaged or defective." In this sense, we can see that aspects of our behavior are out of order. We may blame everyone and everything for our condition instead of taking responsibility for our own behavior problems. If this is our first exposure to Step work, we may be totally unaware of the extent of our condition.

● Which aspects of your behavior are out of order? _____

_____

_____

_____

● What does "restoration to wholeness" mean to you? _____

_____

_____

_____

Many of us have acquired certain behavior patterns and personality traits that we thought would protect us from the painful realities of life. Some of the common behavior patterns are victimization, defiance, self-centeredness and indifference. The presence of these behaviors and attitudes indicates that we suffer from some form of emotional, mental and behavioral disability.

● How do these and other behavior patterns affect your ability to function effectively in your current environment? _____

_____

_____

_____

Some characteristics of our society do not foster or encourage healthy behavior. We are taught from childhood to do what is right. Without adequate moral training, we are expected to know the difference between right and wrong, but based on our early role models, the message as to what is right and wrong was confusing and unclear. As adults, we are expected to behave responsibly and to manage our own lives competently; but in reality, we cannot do so. Frequently, our mistakes are a direct result of the distorted understanding of right and wrong that we acquired in childhood. When we can accept this, we are truly ready to admit that our behavior is ineffective in many areas.

● How did the role models in your life influence your current attitude? _____

_____

_____

_____

● What important traits did your role models lack? _____

_____

_____

_____

Coming to believe in a Higher Power and admitting we behave in a destructive manner require a great deal of humility. Our previous lack of humility contributed greatly to our past ineffectiveness. As we work toward a more balanced lifestyle, we see the importance of humility in all our affairs. Our growth is considerably enhanced by our willingness to be humble and accept our humanness. As we attend meetings and work the Steps, we discover the peace and serenity possible only through surrendering our self-will and humbly seeking to improve the quality of our lives.

- List situations that illustrate your ability to be humble. _____

_____

_____

_____

- List situations that illustrate your lack of humility. _____

_____

_____

_____

Notes: _____

_____

_____

_____

_____

_____

_____

_____

_____

_____

_____

_____

_____

_____

_____

_____

_____

_____

STEP THREE

*Made a decision to turn our will and our lives over
to the care of God as we understood God.*

❧

Step Three requires that we take affirmative action as a result of the developing awareness we have gained from working the first two Steps. In Step One, we admitted we were powerless, that our lives had become unmanageable. In Step Two, we came to believe that a Power greater than ourselves could restore us to wholeness. In Step Three we make a decision to turn our lives over.

- List ways in which Step One prepared you for Step Three. _____
  _____
  _____
  _____

- List ways in which Step Two prepared you for Step Three. _____
  _____
  _____
  _____

Step Three commands more of us than the first two Steps, because we are now asked to trust in a Higher Power. If we feel pressured or compromised by this request we are going too fast. Our inner child may be terrified that, if we dare trust a Higher Power and expose our behavior problems to that Power, we will be rejected. In this case, it is important to stop and take time to prepare ourselves properly. It is through these first three Steps that we set the foundation for working the entire Program and for achieving the peace and serenity we seek.

- What resistance do you feel that indicates you are keeping your Higher Power out of your
  life? _____
  _____
  _____
  _____

- List examples of your willingness to turn your life over to the care of a Higher Power.
  _____
  _____
  _____

The key to effectively working Step Three lies in our willingness to turn as much of our lives as we can over to the care of God. This is difficult for many of us because we are accustomed to functioning by using self-will alone. Our mistrust may have prevented God from having a meaningful place in our lives, and the idea of letting an unrecognized Power be our guide is too unfamiliar to us. We may have learned to pray to God as we would to a celestial Santa Claus, asking for things we wanted and always expecting to receive them. We may have asked for guidance in achieving our worldly goals, but this is vastly different from turning our whole being over to a Higher Power and trusting that we will be safely guided.

● How has mistrust affected your relationship with God? _____

_____

_____

_____

If we have carefully and thoroughly worked Steps One and Two, we have accepted our behavior and are ready to turn our lives over to a new manager. We see that allowing a Higher Power to guide our lives will reduce our fears and resentments to a manageable level. We recognize how that Power's presence impacts our lives as we choose to rely on a Higher Power. We may discover how comforting it is to trust in the outcome, as we see positive changes occurring in our lives.

● What do you expect to happen when you turn your life over to God's management?

_____

_____

_____

We can expect to experience some resistance to turning our lives over to God in the beginning. This can be attributed to our need for independence, since most of us thrive on being in charge and cling to the illusion of being free to "do our own thing." We may relinquish only the parts of our lives that are causing us the most pain. This is a start, and will build our confidence as we see that God can resolve all of our problems. We may be puzzled and confused about what is guidance and what is self-will. Our deepening partnership with a Higher Power clarifies this uncertainty as we accept the step-by-step guidance we receive.

● How does "doing your own thing" interfere with turning your life over to God's care?

_____

_____

_____

● In what ways is your trust in God deepening? _____

_____

_____

_____

Experience tells us that, the more patient we are with ourselves and our growth, the more positive our progress will be. Being patient enables us to more easily grasp the true meaning of recovery. If we try too hard and become obsessed with our desire to get well, our relentless urgency will block our progress, causing frustration, resentment and self-pity.

● Describe how lack of patience has caused problems in your life. _____

_____

_____

_____

The slogan "Let Go and Let God" expresses the central theme of Step Three. The idea of "letting go" and trusting the outcome can be especially helpful when we realize that surrendering our burdens actually frees us to experience healing and growth. As long as we do the appropriate "footwork" and do not expect God to do everything, we will see that our Higher Power takes good care of us.

● What does the statement *"Pray to God, but row toward shore."* mean to you as it relates to

doing the "footwork?" _____

_____

_____

_____

Our distorted thinking, formerly devoted to shoring up our fragile egos, may lead us to believe that we will be ineffective if we turn our will and our lives over to the care of God. Yet, our new experiences prove that the more willing we are to depend on a Higher Power, the more confident we become as we see the direction our lives are taking. Our growing spirituality is reflected in an inner peace—the result of accepting a Power greater than ourselves and following that Power.

● How has depending on a Higher Power increased your confidence in your own abilities?

_____

_____

_____

Caution is an important factor in completing this Step. If we are not completely comfortable with turning our will and our lives over to the care of God, we must slow down and be more reflective. Some of us may be experiencing the intense physical and psychological impact of our ineffective behavior, begun as a way to temporarily numb emotional pain, distract our boredom or relieve our stress. Whatever our behavior involves, whether it be dependency in relationships, inappropriate use of money, drugs or food, we face the prospect of spiritual and perhaps physical death. We began this Program because the path we were taking was interfering with our effectiveness. We needed help to transform our lives and be healed. Being asked to trust in a Higher Power may present a challenge to us until we understand that it is an effective way to improve our lives.

- What ineffective behavior is preventing you from turning your life over to God's care?

  _____

  _____

  _____

The Twelve Steps is a spiritual program—a tool for healing. Step Three is an opportunity to let a spiritual Power greater than ourselves take charge of the rest of our lives. This liberates us from the pressure of feeling responsible for everything and everyone, or expecting someone else to take responsibility for us. As we surrender to our Higher Power and allow others to experience their own Higher Power, we develop a feeling of peace and serenity in our lives.

- How do you see the Twelve Steps as a spiritual program of recovery? _____

  _____

  _____

  _____

It is not important to fully understand how our Higher Power works in order to "let go." We need only to believe in the process to initiate our own growth and thereby enhance our well-being. If we have trouble working Step Three, it is probably because we are having difficulty with the "belief" aspect of Step Two. In this case, we need to return to Step Two before going further.

- What does the statement *"It isn't necessary to understand a Higher Power. We need only to accept that the Power is there and that we can be restored to wholeness."* mean to you?_____

  _____

  _____

- What difficulties are you having with Step Three? _____

  _____

  _____

  _____

When we experience meaningful results in working Step Three, a change comes over us. We are calmer and feel that a weight has been lifted from our shoulders. It can happen suddenly or gradually, as we consciously accept the guidance resulting from our partnership with a Higher Power. If we experience a feeling of euphoria, it will not last forever—at times, we might revert to our old behavior patterns. At this point, we need only to recognize this. There are no saints in this Program—we all have "slips". However, as we work the Program daily, we become more willing and able to turn our lives over consistently.

- List particular instances where you were "successful" in letting go and trusting the outcome. _____

  _____

  _____

  _____

● List particular instances where you were "unsuccessful" in letting go and trusting the outcome. _____

_____

_____

_____

There is a paradox in the way this Program works. The less we try to manage our own lives, the more effective we become. When we give up managing our own lives and trust in our Higher Power's plan for us, we find we are calmer and more accepting of things around us. Friends may compliment us on how well we are managing our lives. As we stop trying to restrict ourselves to a course of rigid self-discipline, people may recognize how at-ease we are in simply being ourselves.

● What changes have you noticed in your behavior that can be attributed to working the Program? _____

_____

_____

_____

● What changes have friends or family members whom you trust noticed in your behavior that can be attributed to working the Program? _____

_____

_____

_____

Most of us start this Program in an effort to stop repeating painful cycles of ineffective and damaging behavior. We are usually in search of answers to the complex questions of life. In the past, some of us may have experimented with lifestyles and beliefs that appeared to offer solutions. We may have been looking for a personal relationship with a Higher Power that transcended things of this world. This life-giving experience is available through the Twelve Step Program.

● What different lifestyles have you experimented with in your search for a better life?

_____

_____

_____

Review your responses to the questions in Step Three and indicate how you have:

● **"Made A Decision..."** List the ways in which you are reluctant to do so. _____

_____

_____

_____

- **"To Turn Our Will And Our Lives Over..."** Explain how turning your life over does not necessarily mean giving up your life. _____

_____

_____

_____

- **"To The Care Of God..."** How do you see your Higher Power as caring for you? _____

_____

_____

_____

- **"As We Understand God..."** What is your current understanding of God? _____

_____

_____

_____

STEP THREE COMMITMENT

I am now willing to enter into partnership with my Higher Power.

"Higher Power, I trust that your
guidance will free me from my ineffective behavior
so that I may better do Your will.
Free me from the personal struggles and difficulties
that are rooted in my dysfunctional family life.
Show me how to love and care for
the precious child within me.
I seek wholeness so that my life may bear witness
to those I would help of Your Power,
Your Love and Your Way of Life.
I seek to do Your Will always."

HIGHER POWER EXERCISE

The purpose of this writing exercise is to deepen your understanding and personal relationship with your Higher Power. This process works best when you can think and write for an uninterrupted period of time. Find quiet, peaceful surroundings with as few distractions as possible.

Don't expect major life-changes to occur as a result of doing this exercise for the first time. You are simply giving yourself an opportunity to renew your relationship with your Higher Power. Your trust in your Higher Power will grow as you calmly and repeatedly reaffirm the existence of that Power.

There are six stages involved in completing this process. Their effect is cumulative, so follow the sequence as listed for best results.

Life Segments

Use the Higher Power worksheet to divide your life into ten-year segments. In each segment, list the heroes you admired, persons you thought to be wise or successful and wanted to imitate. They can be people you have known personally, either living or dead. They can be people you have never known—mythical, historical or religious figures, characters from books, TV or movies.

EXAMPLES: Parents, grandparents, other relatives; saints, priests, prophets, authors, composers, poets, teachers, coaches or political figures.

Briefly describe the uniqueness of each person and note what you hoped to receive or did receive from them.

Special Gifts Received During Life Segments

Transfer the list of special things you received from these figures to the Higher Power worksheet.

Meditation

After completing the above, sit quietly and listen to some quiet music if it is available. Focus on the image of a kaleidoscope. Close your eyes and let all of the entities you have cherished blend together. Don't try to create the emerging image; just let it evolve. It will come to you without any special direction on your part. Accept that the image is forming in your mind at this moment. Relax and allow your own concept of a loving Higher Power to come to you. Creative thoughts present you with an image of all those special people reflected in the light of God's love. Allow your mind to appreciate God's presence as having been a part of the lives of all the people you listed. Imagine your Higher Power's presence with you as you relax and feel quiet, safe, accepted, understood, loved and supported. Your own personal relationship with God is coming to be one in which you can share everything about yourself with no reservations.

Results of Meditation

Slowly open your eyes and return to the present. When you are ready, without interruption, draw a picture or describe in writing the image of your Higher Power that evolved as a result of this experience. List the qualities of that Power that are especially important to you.

Dialogue With Your Higher Power

There is a final step that can be useful in getting in touch with your Higher Power—prayer and meditation. Sometimes a directed meditation is illuminating. One method is to simply relax for a moment and pretend your mind is a tape recorder. Imagine running a cleaning tape through it so that all present thoughts and concerns are erased from your mind. Focus on the loving presence of your Higher Power being with you and filling your mind. Wait for whatever thoughts occur and write them down without judgment. Record spontaneously what you feel. Nothing is irrelevant. Try to capture every word and image that occurs to you. It may seem silly, nonsensical or embarrassing, but write it anyway. Don't think about what you are doing or attempt to make sense of your writing.

When used regularly as an adjunct to prayer and meditation, this exercise will help you focus on the ways that your Higher Power reaches out to you with insight, love and guidance.

Some suggestions that may help you in this process are:

- Avoid looking at the page.

- Close your eyes while writing.

- Ignore punctuation rules.

- Write with non-dominant hand (if you are right-handed, use your left hand) as a means of maintaining spontaneity.

- Allow a dialogue to develop. You are the pen through which your Higher Power is communicating to you.

Limit writing to approximately 15 minutes.

STEP THREE GIFT

Striving for recognition...
Wanting to look good...
Accomplishment...
A relationship that fits my pictures.
All a mirage, relentless...
Thirsting to fill the emptiness within...
Incessantly demanding more
and more.

Yet—ever-present, within,
serene and uncritical...
Poised in the gentle stillness
of infinite patience...
Spirit...
My Higher Power...
Comforting Love...
and Healing
Awaits.

HIGHER POWER WORKSHEET

Life Segments

Example	1-10	11-20	21-30
Grandparent Love Playtime Walks Advice			
31-40	**41-50**	**51-60**	**61-70**

HIGHER POWER WORKSHEET

Special Gifts Received During Life Segments

Love _____   _____

Advice _____   _____

Playfulness _____   _____

_____   _____

_____   _____

_____   _____

_____   _____

_____   _____

_____   _____

_____   _____

_____   _____

_____   _____

_____   _____

_____   _____

_____   _____

_____   _____

_____   _____

_____   _____

_____   _____

_____   _____

STEP FOUR

Made a searching and fearless moral inventory of ourselves.

❧

Our entrance into the Twelve Step Program often occurs after of a series of painful events resulting from reality pushing aside our fantasy world. Our resultant fears and anxieties may have weakened the defenses of our denial system and forced us to look at ourselves, acknowledging the consequences of our behavior. The shock, disbelief and acceptance of the problems in our lives form the foundation for a life-changing adventure that involves self-discovery, healing and recovery. We start by confronting ourselves and uncovering the ineffective behaviors that we developed as part of our social learning. Once we understand that we can change these thoughts, feelings and behaviors, we can then look at the ways in which we have been controlled by them. Our aim is to release their hold on us and to either let them go or, with the help of our Higher Power, transform them.

• What anxieties do you have about admitting your ineffective behavior? _____

_____

_____

_____

• What do you believe is the cause of these anxieties? _____

_____

_____

_____

During the first three Steps, we initiated many changes that have far-reaching effects on our lives. In Step One, we admitted that we were powerless, that our lives had become unmanageable. In Step Two, we came to believe in a Higher Power as a means of restoring our wholeness. In Step Three, we made a decision to turn our will and our lives over to the care of God as we understand God.

• Review Step One and list any areas in which you are having difficulty accepting the idea

of powerlessness and unmanageability. What would help you accept these ideas and re-

duce your anxiety? _____

_____

_____

_____

- Review Step Two and list any areas in which you are having difficulty accepting the idea of a Higher Power and your unhealthy behavior. What is your resistance to accepting yourself just the way you were? _____
  _____
  _____
  _____

- Review Step Three and list any areas in which you are having difficulty accepting the idea of turning your will and your life over to the God of your understanding. What will help you to let go some of your control? _____
  _____
  _____
  _____

Denial is a core component of our illness, and is found in all of us to a greater or lesser degree. It is a destructive aspect of our illness, because it keeps us locked into an increasingly deteriorating pattern of behavior. Denial consists of many complicated defenses and maneuvers that we unconsciously use to prevent ourselves from facing reality. Some recognizable forms of denial are:

- **Simple Denial:** Pretending that something does not exist when it really does (e.g., discounting physical symptoms that may indicate the presence of problems).

- **Minimizing:** Being willing to acknowledge a problem, but unwilling to see its severity (e.g., admitting to estrangement in a relationship when in fact there is overt infidelity).

- **Blaming:** blame on someone else for causing the problem; the behavior is not denied, but its cause is someone else's fault (e.g., blaming your parents for your current inappropriate behavior).

- **Excusing:** Offering excuses, alibis, justifications and other explanations for our own or others' behavior (e.g., calling in sick for a partner when the actual cause of the absence is drunkenness).

- **Generalizing:** Dealing with problems on a general level, but avoiding personal and emotional awareness of the situation or conditions (e.g., sympathizing with a friend's flu symptoms when you know chemical dependency is the underlying cause of the problem).

- **Dodging:** Changing the subject to avoid threatening topics (e.g., becoming adept at "small talk").

- **Attacking:** Becoming angry and irritable when reference is made to the existing condition, thus avoiding the issue (e.g., being unwilling to share your feelings).

- What types of denial do you use to protect yourself from pain and fear? _____
  _____
  _____
  _____

● In what environment is your system of denial most active (e.g., family, work, social relationships)? How is it active? _____

_____

_____

_____

Working the Twelve Steps hels us to become aware of the denial that has protected us from facing reality. In a way, denial has helped to preserve whatever shreds of self-worth and dignity we have maintained. Step Four allows us to look at our denial system, which until now has been one of our major survival techniques. Denial also has distorted our perception and grossly impaired our judgment, rendering us self-deluded and incapable of accurate self-understanding.

● Describe areas of your life where you use denial. _____

_____

_____

_____

● How do you think, feel and behave when you are in denial? _____

_____

_____

_____

An inventory is not a history. It is a list of what is occurring at the moment and does not concern the past. Looking at it this way, the task of creating a fearless inventory is easier, because we have no reason to fear the present. Writing is an especially important element of Step Four and is an essential part of the process. As we list our qualities, we discover the positive as well as the negative aspects of our traits. None of us has all of one and none of the other. It is important to keep a balanced view of our strengths and limitations. Our main goal is to accept what we discover—healing is more likely to occur if we accept ourselves exactly as we are.

● What do you fear about making an inventory? _____

_____

_____

_____

As we more completely understand the origins of our behavior, we may develop an enlightened and mature perspective about being Adult Children. Much of our early trauma was caused by things over which we had no control. We can see how our wounded inner child continues to influence much of our current adult behavior. We can stop engaging in hurtful childish behavior and feeling frustrated when it appears. Step Four uncovers many childhood roots that can be transformed and healed with the help of our Higher Power. Our condition can be compared to that of a gardener who continually lops off the tops of weeds while they persistently continue to grow from the roots. This type of gardening does not complete the job, because it doesn't treat the roots that lie hidden beneath the surface. Turning our lives over to our Higher Power is vital to uprooting the memories that have affected our lives.

- Make a list of your childhood coping behaviors. Which of these do you most often repeat?

  _____

  _____

  _____

- How does understanding your behavior help you to know yourself better? _____

  _____

  _____

  _____

Resentments and fears are catalysts for our problem behaviors. They had a strong impact on the way we acted as children, and we may find them deeply influencing our adult behavior today. Resentment, among other feelings of unexpressed anger, is a source from which many mental and physical ills originate. Going through life with deep resentments can only result in feelings of victimization, discouragement and frustration, as well as poor health. If we allow our resentments to dominate us, we unknowingly give them the power to destroy us.

- List three major resentments you feel toward people, institutions or ideas. _____

  _____

  _____

  _____

The destructive power of fear threatens the stability we seek in recovery. At this point in our recovery, we may find a degree of fear influencing many of our behaviors. Whatever the origin of our fear (e.g., situations of abandonment, criticism or disapproval by authority figures), it can color our thinking and control our behavior, thereby threatening our recovery. As we inventory our fears, we may notice that their presence is particularly pervasive in situations where we believe we have failed or done something wrong.

- List three major fears you have of people, institutions or ideas. _____

  _____

  _____

  _____

Being willing to face our resentments and fears takes courage. However, faith in our Higher Power is the taproot through which we let God come to our aid. The spiritual wasteland that results from resentments and fears can be overcome by sincerely working the Steps in partnership with the guidance of our Higher Power.

- How can strengthening your relationship with your Higher Power help you overcome

  your resentments and fears? _____

  _____

  _____

  _____

Step Four shows us how to look at ourselves and our lives honestly, possibly for the first time. If we do this carefully, a new awareness of ourselves will begin. Our increased sensitivity may help us discover some aspects of our character that are alarming or overwhelming to us. If we have carefully worked Steps One through Three, this discovery should be rewarding.

● What difficulties do you encounter as you look at yourself and your life honestly for the first time? _____

_____

_____

_____

As we prepare our fourth Step inventory, we look at our character traits and review both our limitations and our strengths. Our inability to accept our limitations often produces behavior that is destructive to us and exploits the limitations of others. Our strengths are seen in behaviors that have positive effects on ourselves and others. Before we can seriously work on our problem areas, we need to acknowledge and examine our limitations. Our self-understanding will be accelerated as we discover how we talk to ourselves and others—the ideas, beliefs and attitudes that govern the ways in which we see our world and how we relate to it.

● List at least five traits you consider to be your main strengths. _____

_____

_____

_____

● List at least five traits you consider to be your main limitations. _____

_____

_____

_____

The inventory we are preparing is for our own benefit. It will be the tool for making a major breakthrough in our recovery and setting us on the road to freedom. As we write the inventory, uncomfortable and uneasy feelings may arise. If these feelings make it hard to be completely honest, denial may be at work. If this happens, we can stop for a moment for careful reflection. Reviewing the facts of our personal history will sometimes cause buried feelings to surface. The negative, unwanted and excess emotional baggage we have been carrying can be gradually put aside in light of our new understanding. As we abandon old, useless attitudes, we must remember that our Higher Power is always with us, offering the support and guidance we need to complete this work.

● What feelings do you have as you prepare to do your personal inventory (e.g., fear, anger, judgment)? _____

_____

_____

_____

Notes: _____

_____

_____

_____

_____

_____

_____

_____

_____

_____

_____

_____

_____

_____

_____

_____

_____

_____

_____

_____

_____

_____

_____

_____

_____

_____

_____

_____

_____

_____

_____

_____

_____

_____

_____

_____

_____

IMPORTANT GUIDELINES FOR PREPARING YOUR INVENTORY

The material offered in this Step Four Inventory Guide is somewhat different from the inventory guides used in other Twelve Step Programs. Emphasis is on those feelings and behaviors most commonly found in Adult Children from homes where alcohol-related or damage-inducing behavior was prevalent. When preparing your inventory, choose the traits that specifically apply to you. Don't tackle them all at once. Use recent events and record words and actions as accurately as possible. Take your time. It's better to be thorough with some than incomplete with all.

The inventory begins with exercises on resentments and fears, followed by a series of feelings and behaviors to be examined. This process enables you to prepare yourself for Step Five. You are the primary beneficiary of your honesty and thoroughness in this inventory.

It is important to refrain from generalizing. As you will note in the example provided for "Isolation," being specific helps identify active traits. When you list specific examples, include who, when, where, what. To the best of your ability, give the names of all persons involved in the situation with you (who); record the date the behavior took place (when); indicate the place where this behavior occurred (where); and, finally, describe the feeling or behavior.

RESENTMENT EXERCISE

Our mental and physical ills are frequently a result of our being unaware of our resentments. These feelings become a part of our lifestyles when we lack faith in ourselves and our Higher Power, and feel victimized by life. Learning to deal with resentment in a healthy way is an important part of our recovery process.

List situations in which resentment is a problem for you. Answer the following questions when describing these conditions:

- What or whom do you resent (e.g., people, institutions, principles)?

- What causes you to feel resentful?

- How has this resentment affected the way you think, feel and behave (e.g., lowered self-esteem, diminished goals, difficulty in relationships, physical harm or threats)?

- Which character traits are active (e.g., approval seeking, control, frozen feelings)?

EXAMPLE: **I resent** my boss **because** he doesn't care to hear my explanation of why I am depressed. **This affects** my self-esteem. **This activates** my anger.

- I resent _____

    Because _____

    This affects _____

    This activates _____

- I resent _____

    Because _____

    This affects _____

    This activates _____

- I resent _____

    Because _____

    This affects _____

    This activates _____

- I resent _____

    Because _____

    This affects _____

    This activates _____

- I resent _____

    Because _____

    This affects _____

    This activates _____

FEAR EXERCISE

Our mental and physical ills are frequently a result of our being unaware of our fears. These feelings become a part of our lifestyles when we lack faith in ourselves and our Higher Power, and feel victimized by life. Learning to deal with fear in a healthy way is an important part of our recovery process.

List situations in which fear is a problem for you. Answer the following questions when describing these conditions:

- What or whom do you fear (e.g., people, institutions, principles)?
- What causes you to feel fearful?
- How has this fear affected the way you think, feel and behave (e.g., lowered self-esteem, diminished goals, difficulty in relationships, physical harm or threats)?
- Which character traits are active (e.g., approval seeking, control, frozen feelings)?

EXAMPLE: **I fear** my spouse **because** I can never please him/her. **This affects** my self-esteem. **This activates** my fear of rejection.

- I fear _____

  Because _____

  This affects _____

  This activates _____

  - I fear _____

  Because _____

  This affects _____

  This activates _____

  - I fear _____

  Because _____

  This affects _____

  This activates _____

  - I fear _____

  Because _____

  This affects _____

  This activates _____

  - I fear _____

  Because _____

  This affects _____

  This activates _____

CHARACTER TRAITS (LIMITATIONS)

The example below will assist you in completing the questions asked as part of your Fourth Step Inventory. Follow the suggested guidelines and be as thorough as possible. Refer to **Isolation** in the inventory section for definitions.

ISOLATION

● List specific examples of your behavior that indicate you are isolating yourself; e.g.,

I declined an invitation to Sharon's party last Saturday.

I did not actively participate in the management meeting.

_____

_____

_____

_____

_____

_____

● Identify and explain the underlying causes (fear, resentment, anger, guilt); e.g.,

I am afraid that if I let myself go I will do something foolish. I worry about not fitting in or being conspicuous.

I fear personal criticism if I express myself freely.

_____

_____

_____

_____

_____

_____

● Identify and explain what is being hurt and threatened (self-esteem, goals, security, personal or sexual relations); e.g.,

My self-esteem is affected when I reveal myself to other people. I judge myself without mercy, and I believe they judge me. This interferes with my desire to have a love relationship and to meet new people.

I feel my job security is at risk.

_____

_____

_____

_____

CHARACTER TRAITS (STRENGTHS)

The example below will assist you in completing the questions asked as part of your Fourth Step Inventory. Follow the suggested guidelines and be as thorough as possible. Refer to **Recovery from Isolation** in the inventory section for definitions.

RECOVERY FROM ISOLATION

● List specific examples of your behavior that indicate you isolate less frequently than before; e.g.,

Today I went to lunch with Diane and Evelyn. Although I felt uncomfortable and ill at ease, I was able to share in the conversation. I risked sharing some special feelings about my desire to be in an intimate relationship. I felt less threatened than in the past, because I could see that they were listening, and I trusted they would respect my confidentiality.

During last Monday's management meeting, I expressed a concern relative to increasing business expenses without sufficient increases in sales to cover the expenses. Rather than getting the criticism I expected, I was thanked for providing the insight.

_____

_____

_____

_____

_____

_____

_____

_____

● What do you hope to achieve as you become more confident about situations in which you would usually isolate yourself; e.g.,

I want to cultivate new, healthy relationships that will expand my confidence and help me be more comfortable in social settings. I hope to become more flexible so that I can learn to be spontaneous and have fun.

I want to become more assertive and participate in business settings. I believe this will give me an opportunity to realize my full potential.

_____

_____

_____

_____

_____

_____

_____

_____

REPRESSED ANGER

Anger is a major source of many problems in the lives of Adult Children. It is a feeling that we often repress, because admitting it makes us feel unsafe. In order to protect ourselves in our chaotic homes, we either denied our anger or expressed it inappropriately. Either way, it was safer to protect ourselves by simply pushing our feelings away. We were not aware, then, that repressed anger can lead to serious resentment and depression, which in turn can cause severe physical complications or stress-related illnesses. Today, denying anger or expressing it inappropriately causes problems in our relationships. We may pretend we are happy, because we feel frightened of the consequences that might arise if we express anger.

When we repress anger, we may experience:

Resentment	**Depression**
Self-pity	**Sadness**
Stress/pressure	**Lack of concentration**
Anxiety	**Physical discomfort**

- List specific examples of your behavior that indicate you are angry. _____

_____

_____

_____

_____

_____

- Identify and explain the underlying causes of your difficulty in dealing with anger. ____

_____

_____

_____

_____

_____

- Identify and explain what you feel is being hurt and threatened by your feelings of anger. _____

_____

_____

_____

_____

_____

_____

RECOVERY FROM REPRESSED ANGER

Learning to express anger appropriately is a major step in our recovery. It can prompt the release of other hidden emotions and let others know our hurts and disappointments. We begin to set limits and be honest with ourselves. As we learn to express anger more appropriately, we are better able to cope with our own hostility as well as the hostility of others. Our relationships improve as we begin to feel comfortable expressing ourselves. Stress-related problems diminish, and we even feel better physically.

As we recover from repressed anger, we begin to:

Express anger appropriately   **Set limits for ourselves**
Identify hurt feelings underlying   **Enjoy inner peace**
the anger   **Reduce stress and anxiety**

• List specific examples of your behavior that indicate you can express anger in a healthy way. _____

_____

_____

_____

_____

_____

_____

_____

_____

_____

_____

_____

• What do you hope to achieve as you identify and release your anger? _____

_____

_____

_____

_____

_____

_____

_____

_____

_____

APPROVAL SEEKING

As a result of our dysfunctional upbringing, we fear disapproval and criticism. As children, we desperately wanted to receive love and approval from our parents, grandparents, siblings and significant others. Because this rarely occurred for most of us, we constantly seek validation from others today. However, this need for approval seriously affects the way we pattern our lives and thinking around the needs of others. Not knowing how to love and approve of ourselves, we seek validation from others in order to feel good about ourselves, and may do things to get people to like us. This "other focus" prevents us from discovering our own wants and needs, feelings and desires. We look for reactions in others, assume what we need to do to please them, and then attempt to manage their impression of us. We strive to please everyone and often stay in relationships that are destructive to us so as not to hurt the other person.

When we have a need for approval from others, we may be:

People-pleasing	**Feeling unworthy**
Fearing criticism	**Ignoring our own needs**
Fearing failure	**Lacking self-esteem**

- List specific examples of your behavior that indicate you seek approval from others.

  _____

  _____

  _____

  _____

  _____

  _____

- Identify and explain the underlying causes of your approval seeking. _____

  _____

  _____

  _____

  _____

  _____

- Identify and explain what you feel is being hurt and threatened by your need for approval? _____

  _____

  _____

  _____

  _____

  _____

  _____

RECOVERY FROM APPROVAL SEEKING

As we begin to rely on our own approval and that of our Higher Power, we understand that wanting approval is okay; we learn to ask for it rather than manipulate others to get it. We accept compliments from others and learn to simply say thank you, believing that the compliment is sincere. We focus on our own desires and say "yes" when we mean "yes" and "no" when we mean "no."

As we recover from inappropriate approval seeking, we begin to:

Recognize our own needs   **Be loyal to ourselves**
Tell the truth about how we feel   **Build trust in self and others**

● List specific examples of your behavior that indicate you are not seeking approval only from other people. _____

_____

_____

_____

_____

_____

_____

_____

_____

_____

_____

_____

● What do you hope to achieve as your need for outside approval lessens? _____

_____

_____

_____

_____

_____

_____

_____

_____

_____

_____

_____

CARETAKING

As long as we took care of others, solved their problems and supplied their needs, we did not have time to look at ourselves. As this trait became more pronounced, we completely lost our own identity. As children, we assumed the responsibility for concerns and problems of others that were far beyond our capability to handle and, as a result, were deprived of a normal childhood. The unrealistic demands placed on us and, for some of us, the praise we received for being "little adults" made us believe we had God-like powers. Taking care of others boosted our self-esteem and made us feel indispensable. It gave purpose to our lives. As caretakers, we are most comfortable with chaotic situations in which we are often assured that we are needed. Although we often resent others for taking and not giving, we know only how to give, not receive—we are unable to allow others to care for us. We had no role models to teach us how to take care of ourselves.

As caretakers, we may:

Make ourselves indispensable	**Lose our identity**
Rescue and advise people	**Feel guilty, inadequate**
Ignore our own needs	**Become co-dependent**

● List specific examples of your behavior that indicate you are acting as a caretaker. _____

_____

_____

_____

_____

_____

_____

● Identify and explain the underlying causes of your need to take care of others. _____

_____

_____

_____

_____

_____

_____

● Identify and explain what you feel is being hurt and threatened by your role as a caretaker. _____

_____

_____

_____

_____

_____

_____

RECOVERY FROM CARETAKING

As we put aside the role of caretaker, we become less and less responsible for everyone and everything, thus allowing individuals to find their own way. We give them over to the care of their Higher Power, which is the best source for their guidance, love and support. By dropping the burden of trying to meet everyone's needs, we find time to develop our own interests and lifestyles. Our obsession with caring for others is replaced by an acceptance of the fact that ultimately we cannot control the lives of others. We realize that our main responsibility in life is to our own welfare and happiness.

When we stop being caretakers, we begin to:

Stop rescuing and advising others **Develop our own identity and interests**
Take care of ourselves **Recognize dependent relationships**
Set limits for helping

- List specific examples of your behavior that indicate you are no longer being a caretaker.

_____
_____
_____
_____
_____
_____
_____
_____
_____
_____
_____
_____

- What do you hope to achieve as you become more aware of your own needs and stop being a caretaker? _____

_____
_____
_____
_____
_____
_____
_____
_____
_____

CONTROL

As children, we were victims. We had little or no control over our environment or the events that took place in our lives. As a result, in adulthood, we have extraordinary needs for security and predictability and end up controlling our feelings and behavior, as well as those of others. Our fears create rigidity and prevent us from being spontaneous. We trust only ourselves to complete a task or to handle a situation. We manipulate others to gain their approval and keep a tight rein of control on people and situations that allows us to feel safe. We fear that our lives will deteriorate if we give up our management position and become stressed and anxious when our authority is threatened.

Due to our need to be in control, we may:

Overreact to change	**Be judgmental and rigid**
Lack trust in others	**Be intolerant**
Fear failure	**Manipulate others**

- List specific examples of your behavior that indicate you are attempting to control or manipulate people or situations. _____

_____

_____

_____

_____

_____

_____

- Identify and explain the underlying causes of your need to be in control. _____

_____

_____

_____

_____

_____

_____

- Identify and explain what you feel is being hurt and threatened by your need for control? _____

_____

_____

_____

_____

_____

_____

RECOVERY FROM CONTROL

We become more aware of the way we have attempted to control people and things in order to feel safe and secure. We realize that our efforts have been useless—that others do things their own way and situations have their own ourcomes, in spite of our controlling. We discover more effective ways to meet our needs when we start accepting our Higher Power as the source of our security. As we begin to surrender our wills and our lives to our Higher Power's care, we experience less stress and anxiety. We become more able to participate in activities without being primarily concerned with our own security. Saying the Serenity Prayer is helpful whenever we begin to recognize the reappearance of our need for control.

As we learn to give up control, we begin to:

Accept change	**Reduce our stress levels**
Trust in ourselves	**Find ways to have fun**
Empower others	**Accept others as they are**

● List specific examples of your behavior that indicate you no longer feel a need to be in control. _____

_____

_____

_____

_____

_____

_____

_____

_____

_____

_____

● What do you hope to achieve as you become less controlling? _____

_____

_____

_____

_____

_____

_____

_____

_____

_____

_____

FEAR OF ABANDONMENT

Fear of abandonment is an involuntary reaction to the emotional and/or physical loss of our parents that we experienced in early childhood. As children, we observed unpredictable behavior from irresponsible, emotionally unavailable adults. As their addiction increased in severity, so did their inability to parent. As children, we required more care than they were able to give us; their focus was elsewhere. As adults, we are inclined to choose partners who are also emotionally unavailable. We try to get our "love" needs met by meeting all our partner's needs in order to avoid experiencing the reality and pain of abandonment. "Pleasing," and thereby reducing the possibility of abandonment, takes precedence over dealing with relationship issues or conflicts and produces a tense environment with poor communication.

When we fear abandonment, we may:

Feel insecure	**Worry excessively**
Be people-pleasers	**Feel guilty when standing up for ourselves**
Avoid being alone	**Become co-dependent**

- List specific examples of your behavior that indicate you fear abandonment. _____

  _____

  _____

  _____

  _____

  _____

  _____

- Identify and explain the underlying causes of your fear of abandonment. _____

  _____

  _____

  _____

  _____

  _____

  _____

- Identify and explain what you feel is being hurt and threatened by your fear of being abandoned. _____

  _____

  _____

  _____

  _____

  _____

  _____

RECOVERY FROM FEAR OF ABANDONMENT

As we learn to rely more upon the ever-present guidance and love of our Higher Power, our confidence in our ability to manage our environment increases. Our fear of abandonment diminishes and is slowly replaced by the feeling that we are worthy, lovable and valuable people in our own right. We seek out healthy relationships with people who love and care for themselves. We feel more secure in revealing our feelings and talking about problems in the relationship. We exchange our old fears for trust in our Higher Power and others who show concern for us. We learn to understand and accept a nurturing and loving fellowship within our community. Our self-confidence grows as we begin to realize that, with a Higher Power in our lives, we will never again be totally alone.

As fear of abandonment diminishes, we begin to:

Be honest about our feelings **Consider our own needs in a relationship**
Feel comfortable being alone **Talk about relationship problems**
Express confidence

- List specific examples of your behavior that indicate you no longer fear abandonment.

_____

_____

_____

_____

_____

_____

_____

_____

_____

_____

_____

- What do you hope to achieve as your fear of abandonment lessens? _____

_____

_____

_____

_____

_____

_____

_____

_____

_____

_____

FEAR OF AUTHORITY FIGURES

Fear of people in roles of authority can be a result of our parents' unrealistic expectations of us—wanting us to be more than we were able to be. Their judgmental, critical, blaming style and their inconsistent anger have had an influence on how we interact with others. We see people in authority as having unrealistic expectations of us and fear we cannot meet their expectations. Simple assertiveness displayed by others is often misinterpreted by us as anger or an attempt to control us. This can cause us to feel intimidated, and we may react in our oversensitive and fragile way. In order to avoid confrontation or criticism, we compromise our integrity and values to accommodate those of the person in power. Unable to appreciate how competent we are, we compare ourselves to others and conclude that we are inadequate.

Fear of authority figures may cause us to:

Fear rejection and criticism	**Compare ourselves to others**
Take things personally	**Insist on being right**
Become arrogant to cover up	**Feel inadequate or incompetent**

- List specific examples of your behavior that indicate you fear people in roles of authority.

  _____

  _____

  _____

  _____

  _____

  _____

- Identify and explain the underlying causes of your fear. _____

  _____

  _____

  _____

  _____

  _____

  _____

- Identify and explain what you feel is being hurt and threatened by your fear of authority figures. _____

  _____

  _____

  _____

  _____

  _____

  _____

RECOVERY FROM FEAR OF AUTHORITY FIGURES

As we begin to feel comfortable with people in roles of authority, we learn to put criticism in a more positive light and discover that it can be a tool for learning. We recognize people in authority as being like us, with their own fears, defenses and insecurities. When we stop taking things personally, we will realize how their behavior does not determine how we feel about ourselves. We start evaluating situations and choosing our behavior rather than merely reacting to others. We recognize that our ultimate authority figure is a Higher Power who is always with us.

As we become comfortable with authority figures, we begin to:

Act with increased self-esteem   **Accept constructive criticism**
Stand up for ourselves   **Interact easily with people in authority**

● List specific examples of your behavior that indicate you are gaining confidence around people in authority. _____

_____

_____

_____

_____

_____

_____

_____

_____

_____

● What do you hope to achieve as you become more confident and secure around people in authority? _____

_____

_____

_____

_____

_____

_____

_____

_____

_____

FROZEN FEELINGS

Many of us have difficulty admitting that we have feelings, much less expressing them. As children, our feelings were met with disapproval, anger and rejection. As a means of survival, we learned to hide our feelings or repress them entirely. As adults, we carry stored feelings of pain, guilt, shame and rage deep within us, often unaware of their existence or intensity. We can only allow ourselves to have "acceptable" feelings in order to feel "safe." The way we respond to life and living is distorted in order to protect ourselves from the reality of what we are actually feeling. Distorted and repressed feelings cause resentment, anger and depression, which can, in time, lead to physical illness.

When we have frozen feelings, we may:

Be unaware of our feelings	**Experience depression**
Have distorted feelings	**Develop physical illness**
Repress our feelings	**Have shallow relationships**

- List specific examples of your behavior that indicate you are not expressing your feelings.

_____

_____

_____

_____

_____

_____

_____

- Identify and explain the underlying causes of your inability to express your feelings. __

_____

_____

_____

_____

_____

_____

_____

- Identify and explain what is being hurt and threatened by not expressing your feelings. __

_____

_____

_____

_____

_____

_____

_____

RECOVERY FROM FROZEN FEELINGS

As we get in touch with our feelings and learn to express them, exciting things may begin to happen. Our stress levels decrease as we learn to express our feelings honestly. We learn that expressing our true feelings is a healthy way to communicate and, as a result, we may find others sharing their feelings with us. As we begin to release our stored feelings, we will undoubtedly experience some pain. But as our willingness to allow our feelings to surface increases, the pain lessens, and we find ourselves less frightened and overwhelmed by them. The more willimg we are to risk releasing our emotions, the more capable we will become of having effective and intimate relationships with ourselves, our Higher Power and others.

As we experience and express our feelings, we begin to:

Identify our feelings	**Experience our true self**
Openly express feelings	**Express our needs to others**
Increase intimacy levels	

- List specific examples of your behavior that indicate you are becoming aware of your feelings and are able to express them. _____

_____

_____

_____

_____

_____

_____

_____

_____

_____

- What do you hope to achieve as you become more comfortable with expressing your feelings? _____

_____

_____

_____

_____

_____

_____

_____

_____

_____

_____

ISOLATION

We find it safe in many instances to withdraw from surroundings that are uncomfortable for us. By isolating ourselves, we prevent others from seeing us as we really are. We tell ourselves that we are not worthy and, therefore, do not deserve love, attention or acceptance. We also tell ourselves that we cannot be punished or hurt if we don't express our feelings. Rather than take risks, we choose to hide, thereby eliminating the need to face an uncertain outcome.

When we isolate ourselves, we may be:

Fearing rejection	**Feeling defeated**
Experiencing loneliness	**Self-pitying**
Judging ourselves	**Seeing ourselves as different from others**

- List specific examples of your behavior that indicate you are isolating yourself. _____

_____

_____

_____

_____

_____

_____

_____

- Identify and explain the underlying causes of your desire to isolate. _____

_____

_____

_____

_____

_____

_____

- Identify and explain what you feel is being hurt and threatened by your isolation. _____

_____

_____

_____

_____

_____

_____

_____

RECOVERY FROM ISOLATION

As we begin to feel better about ourselves, we become more willing to take risks and expose ourselves to new people and surroundings. We seek friends and relationships that are more nurturing, safe and supportive than our past relationships. We learn how to participate and enjoy group activities. It becomes easier to express our feelings when we recognize that people will accept us for who we really are. In turn, our self-acceptance and growing self-esteem allow us to experience the precious gift of living more comfortably and serenely.

As we isolate less often, we begin to:

Accept ourselves and others   **Be less self-centered**
Express our emotions   **Actively participate with others**
Cultivate supportive relationships

- List specific examples of your behavior that indicate you isolate yourself less frequently.

_____

_____

_____

_____

_____

_____

_____

_____

_____

_____

- What do you hope to achieve as you feel more confident about situations from which you would usually isolate yourself? _____

_____

_____

_____

_____

_____

_____

_____

_____

_____

_____

LOW SELF-ESTEEM

During childhood, we were never encouraged to believe in our own abilities. As a result of constant criticism, we believed we were "bad" and the cause of our family problems. To feel loved and accepted, we tried harder to please, to be perfect and above reproach. The harder we tried, the more frustrated we became; no matter what we did, we could never please the "big people." We held ourselves in low esteem, affecting our ability to set and achieve our goals. Fearful of making mistakes, we avoid taking risks. We feel responsible for things that go wrong and don't accept credit when something goes right. Instead, we feel undeserving and wait for the "other shoe to drop."

When we experience low self-esteem, we may:

Be non-assertive	**Isolate from others**
Fear failure	**Have a negative self-image**
Appear incompetent	**Need to be perfect**
Fear rejection	

- List specific examples of your behavior that indicate you have low self-esteem. _____
_____
_____
_____
_____
_____
_____
_____

- Identify and explain the underlying causes of your low self-esteem. _____
_____
_____
_____
_____
_____
_____

- Identify and explain what you feel is being hurt and threatened by your low self-esteem.
_____
_____
_____
_____
_____
_____
_____

RECOVERY FROM LOW SELF-ESTEEM

As we work with our Higher Power to see ourselves and our abilities more realistically, our self-esteem increases. We are able to interact with others more confidently and to accept ourselves as we really are, valuing our strengths as well as our limitations. We become more willing to take risks. Recognizing that we can learn from our mistakes, we find we can achieve things we never dreamed possible. We feel safer as we come to know others and allow them to know us. Relationships become healthier, because we are able to trust and validate ourselves and no longer need to look to others for validation.

As our self-esteem increases, we begin to:

Be more confident   **Love and care for ourselves**
Act more assertively   **Openly express feelings**
Interact more easily with others   **Take risks**

- List specific examples of your behavior that indicate your self-esteem is improving. _____

_____

_____

_____

_____

_____

_____

_____

_____

_____

_____

- What do you hope to achieve as you feel better about yourself? _____

_____

_____

_____

_____

_____

_____

_____

_____

_____

_____

_____

OVERDEVELOPED SENSE OF RESPONSIBILITY

As children in a dysfunctional home, we felt responsible for being or creating our parents' problems. We tried to be "model children" and make the problems go away. We believed that we were responsible for the way our parents felt and behaved, even for the outcome of events. Today, we remain super-sensitive to the feelings and needs of others and assume responsibility for creating their feelings and meeting their needs. It is important to us to do our job perfectly. We volunteer to do things so others' lives will be easier and less stressful. This exaggerated sense of responsibility causes us to take on far more than we can handle effectively. We often end up feeling victimized, abused, unappreciated and resentful.

When we are overly responsible, we may:

Take life too seriously	**Be high achievers**
Be inflexible	**Have false pride**
Be perfectionists	**Manipulate others**
Assume responsibility for others	

- List specific examples of your behavior that indicate you are being overly responsible.

_____

_____

_____

_____

_____

_____

_____

- Identify and explain the underlying causes for your being overly responsible. _____

_____

_____

_____

_____

_____

_____

- Identify and explain what you feel is being hurt and threatened when you are overly responsible. _____

_____

_____

_____

_____

_____

_____

RECOVERY FROM OVERDEVELOPED SENSE OF RESPONSIBILITY

Accepting the fact that we are not responsible for the actions and feelings of others forces us to focus on ourselves. We understand that we do not control the lives of others and that people are responsible for themselves. As we assume responsibility for our own thoughts, feelings and actions, we become aware that our Higher Power, not our over-responsible nature, is our source of guidance. In this way, we learn to make the time and find the energy to support and nurture ourselves first, then give appropriately to others.

As we stop being overly responsible, we begin to:

Take care of ourselves   **Accept our limitations**
Enjoy work and leisure time   **Delegate responsibility**

● List specific examples of your behavior that indicate you are not taking responsibility for others. _____

_____

_____

_____

_____

_____

_____

_____

_____

_____

_____

● What do you hope to achieve as you allow others to take responsibility for themselves and begin taking care of yourself? _____

_____

_____

_____

_____

_____

_____

_____

_____

_____

_____

_____

REPRESSED SEXUALITY

We find ourselves confused and uncertain about our sexual feelings toward others, particularly those to whom we are close or those with whom we hope to be emotionally intimate. We have been trained to think of our sexual feelings as unnatural or abnormal. Because we do not share our feelings with others, we have no opportunity to develop a healthy attitude about our own sexuality. As small children, we may have explored our physical sexuality with peers and been severely punished. The message was "sex is dirty, is not talked about and is to be avoided." We may have been molested by a parent or close relative who was out of control. As a result, we are uncomfortable in our sexual roles. We do not freely discuss sex with our partners for fear of being misunderstood and abandoned. We may confuse love with sex and give our bodies indiscriminantly or agree to sex when we really just want a hug. As parents, we may avoid discussing sexuality with our children, thus denying their need for guidance and modeling in the development of their own sexual identities.

Due to repressed sexuality, we may:

Feel guilt and shame	**Use sex to feel good about ourselves**
Lose our sense of morality	**Experience frigidity or impotency**
Be confused about our sexual identities	**Manipulate others by seductive**
Be lustful	**behavior**

• List specific examples of your behavior that indicate you have problems dealing with your sexuality. _____

_____

_____

_____

_____

_____

• Identify and explain the underlying causes of confusion about your sexuality. _____

_____

_____

_____

_____

_____

• Identify and explain what you feel is being hurt and threatened by your inability to express your sexual feelings. _____

_____

_____

_____

_____

_____

RECOVERY FROM REPRESSED SEXUALITY

As we increase our self-love and our ability to take care of ourselves, we begin to appreciate our bodies and our sexual desires as normal and natural. As we seek out other healthy people who love and take care of themselves, we learn to express and ask for affection appropriately. We are less fearful of commitment and better prepared to enter into a healthy relationship— emotionally, intellectually and sexually. We feel more secure in sharing our feelings, desires and limits. Our self-confidence grows and allows us to be vulnerable. We give up the need for perfection in ourselves and others and, in so doing, open ourselves to growth and change. We are honest about our own sexuality with our children. We accept their need for information, as well as their need for healthy sexual identities.

When we accept our sexuality, we begin to:

Communicate appropriately about our sexual needs
Accept our sexual selves

Consider our own sexual needs
Share intimate feelings

- List specific examples of how your behavior is improving. _____

_____

_____

_____

_____

_____

_____

_____

_____

_____

_____

_____

- What do you hope to achieve as you feel more confident with your sexuality? _____

_____

_____

_____

_____

_____

_____

_____

_____

_____

_____

_____

Notes: _____

_____

_____

_____

_____

_____

_____

_____

_____

_____

_____

_____

_____

_____

_____

_____

_____

_____

_____

_____

_____

_____

_____

_____

_____

_____

_____

_____

_____

_____

_____

_____

_____

_____

_____

STEP FIVE

Admitted to God, to ourselves, and to another human
being the exact nature of our wrongs.

❧

When working Step Four, we concentrated on exposing and examining the reality of our lives. If we were honest and thorough, taking inventory was not easy. It took great courage to venture into uncharted waters and face the facts we discovered about ourselves. Step Four usually exposes unresolved feelings, unhealed memories and personality flaws that have caused resentment, depression and loss of self-worth. Following the process carefully enabled us to confront the denial and self-deception that have been "normal" patterns of action and interaction in our lives.

● How thorough do you believe you were in completing your Step Four inventory? Explain.

_____

_____

_____

Thoroughness in the fourth step has helped us to confront the reality of our behavior and the impact it has had on our lives. If we were able to uncover some of the situations that formed our complex behavior patterns, Step Five can be most effective and rewarding. Achieving a balance in the inventory by focusing equally on our limitations and strengths has served to increase our self-awareness and, hopefully, our self-esteem. It has presented us with an opportunity to accept the various aspects of our character. For those who have been honest and thorough, the writing in Step Four has been a gratifying experience, preparing us for Step Five and the many new discoveries to come.

● Which part of your inventory was the most difficult for you? What feelings were present (e.g., anger, sadness, relief)? _____

_____

_____

_____

● Having completed Step Four, what is your current opinion of yourself? How are you focusing on your strengths and being aware of your behavior when your limitations become apparent? _____

_____

_____

_____

It is important to recognize that our relationship with our Higher Power provides the foundation for developing the courage and strength we need to accomplish the healing we seek. Relying on our Higher Power can help us become more willing to take risks, thus making it possible for us to proceed to Step Five. An effective fifth Step is possible only if we are satisfied with our work in Step Four. By making a searching and fearless moral inventory, we are better prepared to face reality and complete the requirements of Step Five.

- In what ways are you experiencing fear or lack of courage in preparing for your fifth Step? _____

_____

_____

_____

- How do you think Step Five can help you recognize and manage your shortcomings? __

_____

_____

_____

Step Five provides a pathway out of our isolation and loneliness. It is a step toward wholeness, happiness and a real sense of renewal. It tests our humility, in the sense that we see ourselves as we really are—one of many human beings, all children of God. As we develop humility, we will feel more secure and self-accepting when admitting to God the exact nature of our wrongs.

- How do you think Step Five will help you bring about effective change in your behavior?

_____

_____

_____

- How has isolating yourself kept you from speaking honestly to yourself and to others?

_____

_____

_____

In Step Five, we admit the exact nature of our wrongs to God, to ourselves and to another human being. It is important to share as much as we possibly can, as the degree to which we cleanse ourselves determines the degree to which we will be ready to proceed with our lives. As our guilt and pain is relieved, we will feel as though a great weight has been lifted from us.

- List any fears that you need to expose before you can successfully complete Step Five.

_____

_____

_____

• Review your Step Four inventory to verify its completeness. Take time now to note what, if anything, has been overlooked. _____

_____

_____

_____

Before proceeding, refer to Guidelines for Preparing Your Fifth Step (page 67).

Step Five provides an opportunity to say things out loud. It may be our first attempt at speaking the truth about ourselves as we now understand it. This can serve to assist us as a future positive communication skill. In completing the fifth Step, our final meeting with another person will first be "rehearsed" by admitting our wrongs to God and ourselves. It can be a rewarding experience.

We begin Step Five by admitting our wrongs to God. This brings us closer to ultimately surrendering to a Higher Power—"Letting Go and Letting God." To attain this goal, we must give up our need to control things and offer ourselves, our desired outcomes and our lives to our compassionate Higher Power. Admitting our wrongs to God is not for God's benefit. It is an opportunity for us to know that our Higher Power loves us and is patiently waiting for us to admit to and learn from our ineffective behavior. In doing this we experience an inner acceptance of our Higher Power and others.

• What method feels most comfortable when admitting your wrongs to your Higher Power? Why? _____

_____

_____

_____

• How do you feel about kneeling to make your admission to your Higher Power? Explain.

_____

_____

_____

Admitting to ourselves the exact nature of our wrongs is the least threatening part of Step Five and can be done with minimal risk. It does not test our honesty or expose our self-deception. Talking only to ourselves prevents us from having to place ourselves in a realistic perspective. Deceiving ourselves is a well-cultivated talent. In the past, we have manipulated our own thoughts and feelings so that we saw only what we wanted to see. However, the admission of our wrongs to ourselves is an important first step in preparing us for our conversation with another human being.

• In the past, how has admitting your shortcomings only to yourself caused you to excuse them or do nothing constructive to alter your behavior? _____

_____

_____

_____

Nothing draws us to each other like honesty and humility. These qualities illustrate our humanity and are truly attractive to others. If we have been humble and honest with God and with ourselves, completing the final stage of Step Five will be relatively easy. Success in this part of Step Five depends on our finding the right person with whom to share ourselves—one with whom we feel comfortable and trusting.

● Describe your experience and resulting feelings when admitting your wrongs to God.

_____

_____

_____

● Describe your experience and resulting feelings when admitting your wrongs to yourself.

_____

_____

_____

● Why is honesty such an important part of acknowledging your faults? _____

_____

_____

_____

The most difficult part of Step Five is admitting our wrongs to another human being. Allowing another person to see parts of us that have been hidden even from ourselves can be a frightening experience. We may be concerned that we will be laughed at or rejected. This Step seriously challenges our ability to be completely honest and willing to accept the consequences.

● What values do you see in admitting your faults to another person whom you respect

and can trust to keep your confidence? _____

_____

_____

_____

● Explain your feelings toward discussing your faults openly with another person. _____

_____

_____

_____

When selecting the person in whom we will confide, we need to look for a dependable person who is familiar with the Program. Trusting the person we choose is essential to feeling safe when we describe ourselves and our behavior. Our ability to share honestly and intimately will be enhanced if we accept our limitations as humans, realizing that none of us is perfect.

- What qualities are important to you as you look for a person with whom to share your fifth Step? _____

_____

_____

_____

When preparing to expose our innermost selves to another person, we need to do more than just talk—we need to be ready, and willing, to listen. If we are willing to listen with an open mind to someone else's viewpoint, we will broaden our awareness and provide ourselves with an opportunity to change and grow. The two-way nature of this encounter is vital to us as a part of our process of self-revelation. Questions and comments shared in a caring and understanding manner often reveal feelings and insights of which we were unaware. We are sometimes amazed to find that other people have experienced painful histories much like our own.

- What can be gained from listening attentively to the other person's viewpoint? _____

_____

_____

_____

We need to be realistic and understand that our longstanding behaviors have become habits that may be extremely difficult to break. Admitting the exact nature of our wrongs does not ensure that they won't be repeated. While we do not plan to have lapses, it is natural to presume that they will occur. Maintaining close contact with our Higher Power will help us to face and deal with them as they happen.

- Describe your feelings after taking Step Five. How have your feelings toward other people changed? _____

_____

_____

_____

- Describe any areas about which you felt uncomfortable while sharing. _____

_____

_____

_____

- As a result of sharing, did you experience an increased level of peace and serenity, or did you experience sadness, anxiety, etc.? Explain. _____

_____

_____

_____

As we complete Step Five, we begin to experience the reality of God's love for us through the way in which our feelings about ourselves are changing. Knowing that our Higher Power is with us helps us make a critical advancement toward healing—that of accepting our humanness.

- In what ways did Step Five bring you closer to God and to others and help you to gain a better opinion of yourself? _____

_____

_____

_____

Notes: _____

_____

_____

_____

_____

_____

_____

_____

_____

_____

_____

_____

_____

_____

_____

_____

_____

_____

_____

_____

_____

_____

IMPORTANT GUIDELINES FOR PREPARING YOUR FIFTH STEP

Choose your Fifth Step listener carefully—one who is familiar with Twelve Step Programs. The individual can be:

- a clergyman ordained by an established religion; ministers of many faiths often receive such requests.

- a trusted friend (preferably of the same sex), a doctor or psychologist.

- a family member with whom you can openly share. Be careful not to disclose information that might be harmful to spouses or other family members.

- a member of a Twelve-Step Program. If you are working with family groups as described in this book, you may find trust already exists and will deepen by doing your Fifth Step with a group member. In some cases, the family group as a whole can be the listener.

In preparing for the Fifth Step, either as communicator or listener, the following suggestions are helpful:

- Begin with prayer, asking your Higher Power to be present as you prepare to go through your Fourth Step revelations and insights. Ask God to guide and support you in what you are about to experience.

- Allow ample time to complete each thought and stay focused on the subject. Discourage unnecessary explanations.

- Eliminate distractions. Telephone calls, children, visitors and extraneous noises should be eliminated.

- Remember that Step Five asks only that we admit the exact nature of our wrongs. It is not necessary to discuss how the wrongs came about or how changes will be made. You are not seeking counsel or advice.

- As the listener, be patient and accepting. You are your Higher Power's spokesperson and are communicating unconditional acceptance.

- As the listener you are there to help the communicator express thoughts clearly. Ask questions when necessary so the information can be clearly understood by both of you.

- When Step Five is completed, both parties can share their feelings about the experience. It is now possible to extend to each other the love our Higher Power extends to us individually.

- Observe confidentiality. What you have shared is personal. Nothing defeats honesty and damages relationships faster than a betrayed confidence.

The following information is helpful when completing your Fifth Step with God:

- Step Five is for your own benefit—your Higher Power already knows you. You are beginning a process of living a life of humility, honesty and courage. The result is freedom, happiness and serenity.

- Imagine your Higher Power sitting across from you in a chair.

- Start with a prayer: e.g., "Higher Power, I understand that you already know me completely. I am now ready to openly and humbly reveal myself to you—my hurtful behaviors, self-centeredness and traits. I am grateful to you for the gifts and abilities that have brought me to this point in my life. Take away my fear of being known and rejected. I place myself and my life in your care and keeping."

■ Speak out loud, sincerely and honestly sharing your understanding of the insights you gained from your Fourth Step inventory. Be aware that emotions may surface as part of the powerful cleansing experience taking place.

■ The objective is balance. Remember that each of your character traits has a strength and a limitation. Begin with resentments and fears, then proceed to those traits you have included in your Fourth Step Inventory.

The following information is helpful when completing your Fifth Step with yourself:

■ Writing your Fourth Step inventory began the process of developing your self-awareness, the first step toward what will become genuine self-love. Solitary self-appraisal is the beginning of your admission, but it is insufficient in itself. The Fifth Step is where you turn that knowledge into enhanced self-acceptance.

■ Sit in a chair facing an empty chair that serves as your imaginary double. Or sit in front of a mirror that allows you to see yourself as you speak.

■ Speak out loud. Allow yourself time to hear what you are saying and to note any deeper understanding that occurs.

■ Acknowledge your courage for proceeding to this point. This and every part of this process releases excess emotional baggage that you have carried around because of low self-worth.

The following information is helpful when completing your Fifth Step with another person:

■ Simply stated, it takes considerable humility to bare ourselves to another person. We are about to reveal our self-defeating, damaging and harmful character traits. We will also disclose our positive and contributing traits. We must do this to remove the stage-characters mask we present to the world. It is a bold step toward eliminating our need for pretense and hiding.

■ Review the guidelines for choosing your Fifth Step listener when selecting a person to assist you in completing your Fifth Step. Begin your sharing with the **Resentment** and **Fear Exercises** in your workbook and then proceed by analyzing the character traits you wrote about.

You may never see that person again, which is okay. It is your decision to continue the relationship in whatever direction you choose, from casual friendship to deeper spiritual companionship.

After completing your Fifth Step, take time for prayer and meditation to reflect on what you have done. Thank your Higher Power for the tools you have been given to improve your life. Spend time rereading the first five Steps and note anything you have omitted. Acknowledge that you are laying a new foundation for your life. The cornerstone is your relationship with your Higher Power and your commitment to honesty and humility.

Congratulate yourself for having the courage to risk self-disclosure, and thank your Higher Power for the peace of mind you have achieved.

STEP SIX

*Were entirely ready to work in partnership with God
to remove our ineffective behavior.*

❧

Our willingness to work Steps One through Five indicates our readiness to complete Step Six. Steps One and Two prepared us for Step Three, at which time we made a decision to turn our will and our lives over to the care of God as we understood God. Steps Four and Five helped us uncover our behavior flaws, facing them courageously and sharing them with God, ourselves and another human being. We have acknowledged our shortcomings and confronted our guilt. Guilt feelings are natural, but clinging to them will halt our progress. We have learned that blaming and punishing ourselves seriously inhibits our growth.

● In what ways have the first five Steps helped you prepare for the removal of your ineffective behavior? _____

_____

_____

_____

Step Six is another opportunity to relinquish our self-will. The partnership and trust we have developed in our Higher Power is the benchmark of our readiness to have our ineffective behavior removed. Most of us have seen healing take place in our lives and the lives of others. Our work to this point has been directed toward cleansing our wounds. We now prepare ourselves to let go and let God help us do the healing that is necessary.

● List behavior changes that indicate your readiness to have God help to remove your ineffective behavior. _____

_____

_____

_____

Our current ineffective behavior stems from many of the traits we have identified. We probably acquired many of these behaviors in childhood, and as adults we continue to use them as a means to survive the chaos and imbalance in our lives. As we become more aware of these behaviors and accept them without fault-finding, we can better deal with them from a position of choice. With the help of our Higher Power, we can use our decision-making ability to perform and express ourselves in a more positive way. Our Higher Power always allows us the freedom to decide how we will deal with our damaging behavior. By being honest with ourselves and our Higher Power, and trusting that we will experience healing, we develop a foundation of strength and hope to draw upon as we meet life's challenges.

- Which feelings surface when you think of surrendering your behavior flaws to your Higher Power and trusting that they will be removed? _____

_____

_____

_____

In our culture, self-will is a highly valued trait. Some of us learned at an early age that we must always strive to improve ourselves. Our parents, teachers and employers emphasized our responsibility to overcome our limitations. As a result, when we accumulate rewards and demonstrate success, we are acknowledged and applauded as being "self-made." It is a rare person who attributes individual success to following the will of a Higher Power.

- How are you relating to your Higher Power at this point in working the Steps? _____

_____

_____

_____

- How much of your progress do you attribute to the strength of your partnership with your Higher Power? _____

_____

_____

_____

It is natural for us to be comfortable with many of our behaviors. Because they have become familiar tools to us, the thought of having them removed can be threatening to our security. As difficult as it may seem, we must be willing to let go of the ineffective behaviors to become "entirely ready" to have God assist us in removing them. Being "entirely ready" requires a dedication much like preparing for a race, learning to speak in front of an audience or developing artistic skills—it requires a lot of practice.

- Identify any disabling behaviors that you are not "entirely ready" to have removed. Explain your attachment to this particular behavior. _____

_____

_____

_____

- List ways that indicate you are willing to accept the notion that God loves you "just the way you are" and is willing to help you remove your ineffective behavior. _____

_____

_____

_____

Preparing to be "entirely ready" to have God help us remove our character flaws is accomplished through systematic repetition of the training we have undergone in the first Five Steps. We have experienced confidence in the ongoing process of working and living the Steps one day at a time. Being "entirely ready" requires faith and belief that our Higher Power knows what we need. As we become willing to relinquish our own self-will and to trust that only the harmful behaviors will be removed, we learn about the gifts God has for us.

● Describe your current level of confidence in working the Steps as a way to improve the quality of your life. _____

_____

_____

_____

The task of removing our ineffective behavior is more than we can handle alone. Step Six does not indicate that we are the ones to do the removing; all we have to do is be "entirely ready" for it to happen. It is a state of being, not something that we actually do. We reach this state of being by faithfully working the Program, whether or not we feel like we are making progress. When we are "entirely ready," our reservations about letting God assist us in removing our shortcomings will have lessened.

● Give an example of how you are inspired by the prospect of working with God to remove your ineffective behavior. _____

_____

_____

_____

With some of the more deeply rooted disabling behaviors, we may find it necessary to move into the role of a "detached observer." By becoming an observer of our behavior and the behavior of others, we can become more aware of how we act or react in various situations. When we see ourselves thinking negatively, or doing something destructive, we can make a note of it and ask for help from our Higher Power. By distancing ourselves as an observer, the task of realizing the depth of our ineffectiveness will become much easier.

● Which ineffective behaviors are going to be the most difficult to give up? _____

_____

_____

_____

● Why are these behaviors so important, and what do you fear you may lose as a result of having them removed? _____

_____

_____

_____

Some people reach a state of preparedness quickly and are ready early in their recovery to help God remove their harmful character traits. However, for most of us the process is a gradual one. Our insecurities may cause us to cling to old habits and unproductive ways of thinking. This blocks the process of change and the flow of inspiration. When this happens, one way to become receptive to God's help with this blockage is to turn to our Higher Power through prayer and meditation.

- How do the Program tools (slogans, prayer, sharing) help you with Step Six? _____
  _____
  _____
  _____

- What is the most effective means through which you turn to your Higher Power for guidance (e.g., prayer, meetings)? _____
  _____
  _____
  _____

It is beneficial to analyze the ways in which we communicate with God. Thinking about the way in which we phrase our statements will illustrate the distinction between asking and admitting. *"Dear God, I want to be more patient"* is making a demand and telling God what we want. *"Dear God, I need help with my impatience"* is simply acknowledging the truth about ourselves. This allows God to make the best decision about how to guide us.

- List examples of your requests and prayers that show you are making demands on God, rather that asking for God's guidance. _____
  _____
  _____
  _____

As we live the principles of the Program in our daily lives, we gradually and often unconsciously become ready to have our ineffective behaviors removed. Our first insight is that we are somehow different—we have changed. The change is often noticed by others before we become aware of it. The approval-seeking person begins to function more appropriately; the control addict becomes warmer and more relaxed; the super-responsible individual is no longer victimizing himself by doing for others what they can do for themselves. People who work the Program as an integral part of their lives become calmer and wear genuinely happy smiles. Much of the change we achieve by working the Program is accomplished without our conscious awareness.

- List the changes in your life that most effectively illustrate your improved behavior. ____
  _____
  _____
  _____

● Which of the **Common Feelings and Behaviors of Adult Children** (page 1) are you over-coming or learning to work with? _____
_____
_____
_____

● Which of the **Common Feelings and Behaviors of Adult Children** (page 1) are still caus-ing you problems and discomfort? _____
_____
_____
_____

A radiant, confident personality exists in each of us, hidden under a shroud of confusion, uncertainty and pain. If someone were to ask us, in our present state of recovery, whether or not we want to be free of our destructive behaviors, we would have only one answer—we are "entirely ready" to help God remove them.

● Describe your understanding of the words "entirely ready." What are your feelings about it? _____
_____
_____
_____

Notes: _____
_____
_____
_____
_____
_____
_____
_____
_____
_____
_____
_____
_____
_____

READINESS EXERCISE

The following exercise is intended to help you prepare to let go of the ineffective character traits you discovered when working Step Four. When necessary, refer to your Fourth Step written inventory.

Pride: Inordinate conceit; disdainful behavior or treatment of others.

- List examples that indicate you are willing to let go of your constant need to impress others. _____

_____

_____

_____

- What difficulty are you having in letting go of your preoccupation with self? _____

_____

_____

_____

Greed: Selfishness; excessive acquisitiveness; never having enough of anything.

- What do you fear you will lose by letting go of your intense desire for material things?

_____

_____

_____

- What will you gain by giving up your selfish tendencies? _____

_____

_____

_____

Lust: Lechery; an intense indulgence in inappropriate sexual activity.

- What inappropriate sexual behavior will you be giving up? _____

_____

_____

_____

● How will removing your lustful tendencies change your current social behavior? _____

_____

_____

_____

Dishonesty: Deceit; disposition to defraud or deceive; justifying behaviors by explaining ourselves dishonestly.

● What anxieties do you feel when you realize the need to tell the truth? _____

_____

_____

_____

● How will honesty improve the quality of your life? _____

_____

_____

_____

Gluttony: Covetousness; one given habitually to greedy or voracious acquisition of possessions; excessive eating or drinking.

● In the process of changing your habits of over-indulgence, what benefits do you hope to

receive? _____

_____

_____

_____

● What are you ready to give up? _____

_____

_____

_____

Envy: Jealousy; painful or resentful longing for an advantage or benefit enjoyed by another, joined with a desire to possess the same perceived benefit.

● In what ways are you ready to lessen your desires for status and material wealth? _____

_____

_____

_____

● What do you believe your life will be like when you no longer experience jealousy? ____

_____

_____

_____

Laziness: Disinclined to activity or exertion; not energetic or vigorous; distinct avoidance of responsibility.

● List examples that indicate you are willing to heighten your productivity. _____

_____

_____

_____

● What steps have you taken to eliminate your habit of procrastination? _____

_____

_____

_____

STEP SEVEN

Humbly asked God to help us remove our shortcomings.

❧

Attaining greater humility is the foundation of the Twelve Step Program. Through acceptance of ourselves, our strengths and our limitations, we develop the desire to seek and do God's will. Working and living Steps One and Two required a degree of humility so that we would admit our powerlessness and come to believe that a Power greater than ourselves could restore us to wholeness. In Step Three, humility allowed us to turn our will and our lives over to the care of God as we understood God. Without humility, Steps Four and Five would have been extremely difficult. In Step Six, our degree of readiness to have our ineffective behaviors removed was directly proportionate to our degree of humility.

● What is your definition of humility? _____

_____

_____

_____

● How have you practiced humility while working the Steps? _____

_____

_____

_____

The emphasis in Step Seven is on our ability to develop and practice humility. This occurs as we develop conscious contact with our Higher Power and regularly seek guidance in the affairs of our lives. Shifting our focus enables us to have our needs met in a healthy non-codependent way. This shift produces harmony with our Higher Power and other people. As we grow in the Program, we begin to understand that humility is a necessary ingredient for our healing. Only by a deepening understanding of this requirement can we adequately prepare to ask God's help in removing our shortcomings.

● Give examples of how being humble helps you focus less on your will being done and more on that of your Higher Power. _____

_____

_____

_____

We seek humility because we realize it is the only way to achieve peace, serenity, happiness and manageability in our lives. Our desire to be a maturing, growing, useful and joyous person requires an inner calm, even in a turbulent, unbalanced world. Learning to accept things we cannot change, and to ask God for the courage to change the things we can, will help us achieve these desires.

- Describe a recent event that prompted you to use the Serenity Prayer to experience inner calm. _____

_____

_____

_____

Humbly asking God to help remove our shortcomings does not necessarily mean that they will all disappear at one time. They are usually shed one by one, so it is important to deal with them individually, preferably with the easiest ones first, so that we build confidence in our progress. Our commitment to working the Program one day at a time supports the idea that with God's help, progress will come at a comfortable pace. If we ask God to remove an ineffective behavior and it is not immediately removed, becoming discouraged or angry is inappropriate. We need to be patient and realize that we have more work to do. We may not be entirely ready to release the particular defect we are focusing on, or we may not have humbly asked God for help.

- What does *"Humbly asked God to help us remove our shortcomings"* mean to you? _____

_____

_____

_____

- What are some shortcomings that you feel justified in keeping? Explain. _____

_____

_____

_____

Positive preparation for removing our shortcomings demonstrates our willingness to let go of our destructive behaviors and cooperate with our Higher Power in the healing process. We cannot expect our circumstances to change if we continue to behave in ways that are hurtful to ourselves and others, while simply waiting for God to do all the work. Even though we have turned it over to God and have asked for help, we should be aware of our tendency to repeat old behaviors. If we do become aware of "old behaviors" at work, we can simply observe them and not be overly judgmental with ourselves. God loves us the way we are, and the realization that we are repeating destructive behavior patterns is an opportunity for us to forgive ourselves as God forgives us.

- What situations trigger your behaving in the "old" manner? _____

_____

_____

_____

- Cite examples of being overly judgmental with yourself. What do you believe is causing this (e.g. low self-esteem, perfectionism)? _____

_____

_____

_____

When reflecting on the recurrence of behaviors that we consider destructive or "immature," it is wise to remind ourselves that our inner-child has not matured. With our love and parenting, the wounded child within us can evolve spiritually, mentally, emotionally and behaviorally. Any improvement, however small, is cause for gratitude and joy. Remember that this process of spiritual development is designed to last a lifetime, yet we practice it one day at a time—or one minute at a time when necessary.

- In what areas do you see yourself as "immature"? _____
  _____
  _____
  _____

- How do you acknowledge yourself for the progress you have made in handling situations
  with more maturity? _____
  _____
  _____
  _____

No matter how hard we try, we can never hope to eliminate all the negative thoughts or ineffective behaviors from our lives. In spite of all the praying we do for guidance, we may sometimes react inappropriately and cause pain to ourselves and others. Achieving sainthood is not a part of this Program. We simply do the best we can, understanding and accepting our humanness without catering to it. Our intentions may be good, but they do not protect us from occasional lapses. We need only to acknowledge our limitations and humbly ask God for help in removing our shortcomings.

- In what ways have you become more patient with yourself as a result of working the
  Program? _____
  _____
  _____
  _____

Letting go of old negative behavior patterns, however destructive they may be, can create a sense of loss and require time to grieve. It is normal to grieve the loss of something we no longer have. If, in our childhood, people or "things" were taken from us before we were ready to release them, we may be overly sensitive and thereby resist experiencing the feelings that accompany the loss of familiar behaviors. Rather than using our own ineffective strategies to avoid or deny our fears, we can turn to our Higher Power for help and support. Even though our childhood learning did not adequately prepare us to handle the grieving for adult losses, our love and trust in God can heal our memories, repair the damage and restore us to wholeness.

- What "things" were taken away from you in your youth before you were ready to give
  them up? _____
  _____
  _____
  _____

● What important person(s) abandoned you emotionally or physically in childhood? How has this contributed to your fear of abandonment or rejection in your adult relationships? _____

_____

_____

_____

Approaching Step Seven, we realize that we have entered into a natural "partnership" with our Higher Power—with healing and wholeness as its primary aim. In this partnership, we cannot take credit for the actual removal of our ineffective behavior. We can credit ourselves with the "footwork" necessary for that removal and our Higher Power with the support and guidance we receive. Changes will occur, but perhaps not how we expected, or in our desired time frame. God assists us in removing our character flaws when we are ready. When we humbly ask God to do the removing, we are not responsible for the outcome, but we are responsible for the preparation—for being "entirely ready."

● What is your reaction to the idea that God may not remove *all* your ineffective behavior?

_____

_____

_____

● What is your reaction to the idea that your shortcomings cannot be removed until you are ready to give them up? _____

_____

_____

_____

The items remaining in our inventory after completing this process are there for a reason. We have an opportunity to accept these remaining negative behaviors and allow God to transform them into positive traits. This can be a rewarding and exciting experience. Leaders may be left with a quest for power but with no desire to misuse it. Lovers may be left with exquisite sensuality but with enough sensitivity to refrain from hurting those they love. The materially wealthy may continue to be, but will set aside their greed and possessiveness.

● What negative qualities remaining in your inventory have the potential to become positive traits? _____

_____

_____

_____

Practicing the Steps on a daily basis until they become routine will help us reach our goals of peace, serenity, happiness and manageability. By doing so, we will eventually be capable of breaking the hold that our old habits and behaviors have had on our lives. We will begin to trust the thoughts and feelings we have that are a result of our conscious contact with God. We will learn that the guidance we receive from our Higher Power is always available; all we need to do is listen and act in spite of our fear.

- In what way are you practicing the Steps on a daily basis? _____
  _____
  _____
  _____

- How do you feel about practicing the Steps daily? _____
  _____
  _____
  _____

STEP SEVEN COMMITMENT

"Dear Higher Power,
I am "entirely ready" to let go of
that which is in me and interferes with
my cooperating in doing your work.
I humbly seek to be restored to wholeness;
to love and to be sensitive to my inner-child
and to relate to others in a wholesome way.
My life is yours,
as I continue to do your bidding.
Thank you for helping to heal me.

SERENITY PRAYER

"God, grant me the serenity
to accept the things I cannot change,
the courage to change the things I can,
and the wisdom to know the difference."

TRAIT REMOVAL EXERCISE

The following exercise is intended to help you review your success in letting go of your ineffective character traits.

Humility: Being aware of one's shortcomings; not proud; not aggressive; modest.

- List ways in which you are practicing humility. _____
  _____
  _____
  _____

- How has humility helped your willingness to have God remove your shortcomings? ____
  _____
  _____
  _____

Generosity: Willingness to give or share; being unselfish.

- Cite examples of your willingness to share with others. _____
  _____
  _____
  _____

- How does your new behavior help you to care about the happiness and welfare of others?
  _____
  _____
  _____

Acceptance of Sexual Self: Feeling comfortable with your sexual nature, without needing to have it lead to sexual intercourse. Clearly expressing preferences for sexual activity with partner.

- How has your sexual behavior improved as a result of letting go of your inappropriate
  sexual relating? _____
  _____
  _____
  _____

- How has your self-esteem been enhanced because of your improved sexuality? _____

_____

_____

_____

Honesty: Telling the truth; being trustworthy.

- What feelings surface when you risk being honest in your communication with other people? _____

_____

_____

_____

- How has being trustworthy improved your relationship with others? _____

_____

_____

_____

Temperance: Moderation in eating and drinking; control of self-indulgence in all things.

- Cite examples which indicate moderation in your use of food and drink. _____

_____

_____

_____

- How do you control self-indulgence in other areas? _____

_____

_____

_____

Amicable: Friendly; harmonious; enthusiastic and helpful toward others.

- How has being friendly helped you to feel more comfortable with yourself and others?

_____

_____

_____

- List ways in which your enthusiasm toward others is improving your self-confidence. ___

  _____

  _____

  _____

Energetic: Active interest in ideas and activities; attention to needs at work and play.

- In what areas of your life has increased energy been most rewarding? _____

  _____

  _____

  _____

- Cite examples of your work habits that indicate you are being more productive. _____

  _____

  _____

  _____

SERENITY PRAYER EXERCISE

The following examples are intended to help you in using the Serenity Prayer as part of your ongoing recovery process. It is a tool that can be used daily when seeking God's help. The exercise gives you an opportunity to take a situation through the Serenity Prayer.

God, grant me the serenity to accept the
things I cannot change . . . .   I can't make _____ like me and praise me.

the courage to change the things I can . .   I can change the way I think and feel about myself.

and the wisdom to know the difference . .   between the satisfaction of giving myself love and approval and the temporary satisfaction of depending on _____ for it.

God, grant me the serenity to accept the
things I cannot change . . . .   the way I was victimized as a child.

the courage to change the things I can . .   my current feelings about being victimized.

and the wisdom to know the difference . .   between having to do something to survive and being able to choose how I feel and act.

Select a specific situation or condition in your life that is currently a source of resentment, fear, sadness or anger. It may involve relationships (family, work or sexual), work environment, health or self-esteem.

God, grant me the serenity to accept the things I cannot change

● State the condition, experience or persons of which you are aware that you cannot change (e.g., childhood, partner's behavior, employment conditions, parents' behavior). _____

_____

_____

_____

The courage to change the things I can

● Indicate what you believe you can change. _____

_____

_____

_____

And the wisdom to know the difference

- Identify your understanding and acceptance of what you can and cannot change (e.g., frozen feelings vs. flowing feelings; anger vs. peace). _____
_____
_____
_____

- List any insights gained from this exercise. _____
_____
_____
_____

Notes: _____
_____
_____
_____
_____
_____
_____
_____
_____
_____
_____
_____
_____
_____
_____
_____
_____
_____
_____
_____
_____
_____

STEP EIGHT

*Made a list of all persons we had harmed, and
became willing to make amends to them all.*

❧

Step Eight brings us to the end of isolation from ourselves, our community and our
Higher Power, and sets the course for restoring our relationships. We release the need
to blame others for our misfortune and accept responsibility for our own lives. Our Step
Four inventory revealed how our behavior caused injury to us as well as to others. In Step
Eight, we document our personal conflicts with others, citing the dates and listing the names
of all the people involved. We cannot effectively change our behavior until we look at our
past and eventually make restitution where needed. This is accomplished through careful
examination and thoughtful analysis of what happened, when and to whom.

● How do you see Step Eight as a design for improving your relationships with others?

_____

_____

_____

The first seven Steps are personal, in that they focus on examining our past behavior patterns
and making us aware of our personal strengths and limitations. Step Eight begins the process
of making adjustments to our lives as a result of what we have discovered in the previous
Steps. By the time we reach this point in recovery, we realize how important it is for us to
let go of the painful memories of our past and the circumstances surrounding them. Releasing the past opens the door to healing and to a new life for us, a life based on living one day
at a time in harmony with ourselves and others.

● List three personal experiences that require making amends. _____

_____

_____

_____

● How can making these amends help to release the past? _____

_____

_____

_____

To find fulfillment in recovery, we first learn to identify our feelings of guilt, shame, resentment and low self-worth, as well as fear of situations and other people. Once we identify these feelings, we then ask our Higher Power for help in removing them. This may seem like an awesome task, because we probably have been controlled by these negative feelings for as long as we can remember. Now, for the first time, we have an opportunity to experience a sense of personal integrity and self-authority by working the Steps. We can put our faith and trust in this process, because it has worked miracles for millions of people.

- How can making amends help remove your guilt, shame and resentments? _____
  _____
  _____
  _____

- How can making amends help increase your self-esteem and improve your interaction with others? _____
  _____
  _____
  _____

The first part of Step Eight specifically states that we list those persons whom we have harmed. When making the list, many of us may encounter a wall of resistance. It can be a severe shock to realize that we must make face-to-face admissions of our past wrongs to those with whom we have had conflict. It was humiliating enough to admit our wrongs to ourselves, to God and to another human being in Step Five. In Step Nine, we will actually make direct contact with the people concerned.

- List actions or experiences you believe were harmful to yourself or to others. _____
  _____
  _____
  _____

If we have conscientiously worked the first five Steps, we are usually aware of the harm we have caused to others by the time we reach Step Eight. We may even see that we have become our own worst enemies, by allowing our attitudes toward ourselves to create excessive self-blame, guilt and shame. Guilt is remorse over having done or not done something we believe to be important. It is often an appropriate response to the regret we feel for actions or inactions that conflict with our personal values. Shame is a feeling of being deeply flawed or defective as a person, and causes us to view ourselves as bad or worthless. These are all unhealthy views of ourselves that can lead us into severe depression.

- List the ways in which you believe you have harmed yourself. _____
  _____
  _____
  _____

We start Step Eight by making a list of the people with whom we feel uncomfortable. We make the list without being concerned about the details; simply making the list enables us to follow where our mind takes us. The list may include family members, business associates, friends, creditors, neighbors. Its length is not important, yet the list may reveal a somewhat unrealistic view of what we believe to be the power of our own personal influence. Step Eight prepares us for the ongoing process of healing that this Program offers. Our willingness to risk honesty enables the healing to take place.

● Examine the list of people you have harmed. Identify what you have done most frequently that caused physical, emotional, mental or spiritual harm. _____

_____

_____

_____

● Name the people on your list to whom you feel the greatest need to make amends? Why? _

_____

_____

_____

Step Eight asks that we face the truth of our behavior and become willing to make amends. We also should be prepared to willingly accept the consequences and take whatever measures are necessary to make restitution. This means fully and completely acknowledging our part in the circumstances where someone was harmed as a result of our action or inaction. Accepting responsibility and making appropriate restitution are vitally important activities. Only through expressing genuine regret for our behavior can we complete the housecleaning necessary for putting the past behind us and achieving the peace and serenity we desire.

● Identify any reluctance you have toward making amends. What might be causing the
reluctance? _____

_____

_____

_____

● What is your feeling about making amends (e.g., anxiety, hope, doubt)? _____

_____

_____

_____

Willingness is the next key element in completing Step Eight. Being willing to forgive ourselves, as well as those who have caused us harm, is an important aspect of this process. This may require a great deal of humility from us. We are already aware that having resentments and holding grudges are luxuries we cannot afford—they not only destroy our serenity and well being but they are more harmful to us than to the persons we resent. Harboring a resentment or grudge is like having an open wound eating away at us. It causes discomfort and makes us angry, bitter and ill-tempered. These feelings can deplete our energy, making us very difficult to be around.

- In the process of preparing to make amends, have you begun to feel that you can forgive yourself? How does this give you courage to continue working this Step? _____
  _____
  _____
  _____

- How are resentments and grudges interfering with your willingness to make amends?
  _____
  _____
  _____

In the past, we were engrossed in our problems and incapable of examining our interaction with others. We became resentful, blaming and revengeful. An effective means of overcoming our resentments and hurtful feelings is recognizing that we are not always victims of circumstances—we have a responsibility for what happens in our lives. Accepting this level of responsibility demonstrates that we have reached a new level of compassion and understanding toward ourselves and others. It shows our willingness to actively pursue the possibility of change and improvement in our behavior. Through acceptance, forgiveness and turning to our Higher Power for guidance, we can let go of our need to hang onto feelings about old issues that may never be resolved.

- What part does your Higher Power play in your preparation for making amends? _____
  _____
  _____
  _____

Step Eight helps us identify the damage we have done and prepares us for Step Nine. Our continued growth requires that we make amends, in order to reduce the likelihood of repeating our unhealthy patterns of behavior. A forgiving attitude will assist us with this work. If we do not accept and forgive ourselves, we cannot accept and forgive others. If we do not accept and forgive others as they are, we cannot make amends with dignity, self-respect and humility. Making amends without extending forgiveness is meaningless and can lead us into further arguments or disputes. Our capacity to make amends must stem from a sincere desire to forgive and be forgiven.

- Why is forgiving yourself a key factor in completing this Step? _____
  _____
  _____
  _____

When looking at those we have harmed, we see that our ineffective behavior played a major part in sabotaging our lives and our relationships. For example:

- When we became angry, we often harmed ourselves more than others. This may have resulted in feelings of depression or self-pity.
- Persistent financial problems resulting from our irresponsible actions caused difficulty with our family and our creditors.

- When confronted with an issue about which we felt guilty, we lashed out at the other person rather than look honestly at ourselves.

- Frustrated by our lack of control, we behaved aggressively and intimidated those around us.

- Because of our indiscriminate sexual behavior, true intimacy was impossible to achieve or maintain.

- Our fear of abandonment sometimes destroyed our relationships, because we did not allow others to be themselves. We created dependency and tried to control their behavior in an effort to maintain the relationship as we wanted it to be.

● Which harmful behaviors caused injury to yourself or to others? _____

_____

_____

_____

● What feelings are you aware of in responding to the above question? _____

_____

_____

_____

Practicing humility will help us see that other human beings have an equal right to live the life of their choice. This does not mean we have to agree with everyone about everything, but that we can choose to stop resenting, hating and wishing harm to people because their views are different from ours. Our own sanity will be preserved, and our serenity greatly enhanced, if we can forgive and extend goodwill to those who disagree with us.

● Explain why humility is necessary for the completion of Step Eight. _____

_____

_____

_____

As we proceed through the Steps, we can indeed learn to forgive, like and even love those whose values differ from ours. In doing so, we will understand the conflicted and oppositional part of ourselves. If we are willing to make amends and face our past, we will become more tolerant and forgiving, less rigid and judgmental. As this happens, we gradually realize that our Higher Power is doing for us what we could never do for ourselves. As our viewpoints, attitudes and beliefs change, we can participate in the process of reconciliation and move on to Step Nine, actually making the amends that are necessary.

● How will forgiving those whose values differ from yours contribute to your healing? __

_____

_____

_____

- List ways in which your changing attitudes are allowing healthy relationships to develop.

  _____

  _____

  _____

AMENDS LIST GUIDELINES

The following are three main categories in which we may have caused harm and for which we may want to make amends.

Material Errors: Actions which affected an individual in a tangible way, such as:

- Borrowing or spending extravagance; stinginess; spending in an attempt to buy friendship or love; withholding money in order to gratify yourself.
- Entering into agreements that are legally enforceable, then refusing to abide by the terms or simply cheating.
- Injuring or damaging persons or property as a result of our actions.

Moral Errors: Inappropriate behavior in moral or ethical actions and conduct, including questions of rightness, fairness or equity. The principal issue is involving others in our wrongdoing:

- Setting a bad example for children, friends or anyone who looks to us for guidance.
- Being preoccupied with selfish pursuits and using other people in the process.
- Inflicting moral harm (e.g., sexual infidelity, broken promises, verbal abuse, lack of trust, lying).

Spiritual Errors: "Acts of omission" as a result of neglecting our obligations to God, to ourselves, to family and to community.

- Making no effort to fulfill our obligations and showing no gratitude toward others who have helped us.
- Avoiding self-development (e.g., health, education, recreation, creativity).
- Being inattentive to others in our lives by showing a lack of encouragement to them.
- Forgetting birthdays, holidays and other special occasions.

AMENDS LIST

Person	Relationship	My Errors	Effect on Others	Effect on Me
Joan	wife	angry insults	fear, anger	guilt, shame
John	co-worker	sexual advances at party	distrust, shame	loss of self-respect

AMENDS LIST EXERCISE

Select the person to whom you have caused the most harm and answer the following questions.

Name: _____ **Harm:** _____

- What is the reason for making the amend? _____
  _____
  _____
  _____

- If you have resistance to making the amend, what is it? _____
  _____
  _____
  _____

- How do you feel about making the amend? _____
  _____
  _____
  _____

- What ineffective behaviors were demonstrated in your relationship with this person? ___
  _____
  _____
  _____

- Describe your willingness to ask for forgiveness and accept the consequences. _____
  _____
  _____
  _____

- When and how do you plan to make the amend? _____
  _____
  _____
  _____

Notes: _____

_____

_____

_____

_____

_____

_____

_____

_____

_____

_____

_____

_____

_____

_____

_____

_____

_____

_____

_____

_____

_____

_____

_____

_____

_____

_____

_____

_____

_____

_____

_____

_____

_____

_____

_____

_____

_____

STEP NINE

Made direct amends to such people wherever possible,
except when to do so would injure them or others.

❧

Step Nine is another action step and requires that we confront issues from our past that may have been dormant for a long time. This Step clearly requires courage, as well as a renewed dedication to freeing ourselves from the guilt we feel about inflicting injuries upon others. The extraordinary life-restoring benefits we will receive greatly compensate for the risk of making amends.

● What does "making direct amends" mean to you? _____

_____

_____

_____

● Explain why reviewing each situation to determine fault is unnecessary. _____

_____

_____

_____

The painful memories, which still may be fresh in our minds, can encumber us. They seriously affect our vitality and impair our joy for living. Making amends can divest these memories of their power and ability to affect our present thoughts, feelings and behaviors. Making amends to a person with whom we have had an uncomfortable experience can be compared to the release of a butterfly trapped in the hands of a curious child. Letting go gives both parties the opportunity to explore and move about independently and naturally; a new relationship now exists between them. Each person can redefine their own role and move toward greater interdependence and comfort in the relationship.

● How do you see forgiveness as setting you free and releasing your painful memories?

_____

_____

_____

Clear judgment, courage and determination are qualities we need when taking Step Nine. It is wise to reflect carefully upon the amends we intend to make. Our objective is not to gain peace of mind at the expense of causing grief to others, but to obtain it in a way that is beneficial for all parties. Forethought and sensitivity will help us decide on an appropriate time, place and form in which to make our amends. It will also help us find ways to keep from causing further harm. We also may choose to seek guidance from a trusted friend, and ask our Higher Power for support in this process.

- Why is it important to take time for careful reflection prior to making amends? _____

  _____

  _____

  _____

Step Nine requires that direct amends be made wherever possible. We may procrastinate by telling ourselves the time is not yet right. We may be tempted to skip the more humiliating and dreaded meetings, or to make excuses to avoid the meetings. We may delay because we are afraid; it is a fearful step we are about to take. Our fear is normal and natural, as we are facing an unknown outcome. We can turn the outcome over to our Higher Power, trusting that we will benefit from whatever happens. We also can rely on the courage of our Higher Power, when we have none. Accepting the consequences of our past behavior and taking responsibility for the impact we have had on others are the core and essence of Step Nine.

- How can you receive the strength to make these direct amends from a supportive and

  loving friend? _____

  _____

  _____

  _____

- When making amends, how will you be certain that lingering resentments will not prevent your amends from being meaningful? _____

  _____

  _____

  _____

Amends will be possible with almost everyone, even those who may not be aware of the harm done, since we can inflict harm by thoughts and words as well as by actions. If someone is unable to accept our apology and restitution, their part of the problem will have to remain unresolved. Our only responsibility is to make sincere amends. In these instances, the Serenity Prayer will help to restore and preserve our peace of mind.

- How can you use prayer and meditation before making direct amends? _____

  _____

  _____

  _____

When preparing to make amends, we see that there are various categories into which amends fall. They are:

People who are readily accessible and can be approached as soon as we are ready.

These include family members, creditors, co-workers and others to whom we owe an amend, and may involve friends as well as enemies. It is harder to approach an enemy than a friend, but we may find it more beneficial. When we are ready to face the consequences of our shared past, we will be able to go to anyone, admit the damage we have done and make restitution. The generous response of most people to such sincerity may astonish us. Not infrequently, our severest and most determined critics will meet us more than halfway on our first attempt.

- Which people on your amends list fall into this category? _____
  _____
  _____
  _____

- What are the risks you take by making amends to these people? _____
  _____
  _____
  _____

Situations that will not allow us to make direct personal contact.

These refer to those who are no longer accessible, are deceased, or might be further harmed by our amend (e.g., someone already in poor emotional or physical health). In these cases, indirect amends can satisfy our need for reconciliation. We can make indirect amends through prayer or by writing an unmailed letter, as if we are actually communicating with the absent person. Indirect amends to family members can be made by sharing our amend with, or doing a special kindness for, someone else's child or parent, when we no longer have the opportunity to do it for our relative. We can make important amends to our adult children by respecting their adulthood and maintaining our own recovery as healthy adults, both physically and emotionally.

- Which people on your amends list fall into this category? _____
  _____
  _____
  _____

- How will prayer or writing help you make amends when direct contact is not possible?
  _____
  _____
  _____

People to whom we can make only partial restitution because complete disclosure could cause harm to them or others.

These people may include spouses, ex-partners, former business associates or friends. We must analyze the potential harm to them should complete disclosure be made. This is especially true in cases of infidelity or promiscuous behavior. Amends in this area can cause irreparable damage to all parties involved. Even in cases where the matter can be discussed openly, we should be extremely careful to avoid harming third parties. Making the burdens of others harder to bear does not lessen our burden. Amends for unfaithfulness can be made indirectly by changing behavior or by concentrating sincere affection and attention on the one who has been deceived.

- Which people on your amends list fall into this category? _____

_____

_____

_____

- How do you intend to make amends without causing harm? _____

_____

_____

_____

In cases involving serious consequences, such as potential loss of employment, imprisonment or alienation from one's family, we need to weigh the consequences carefully. We should not be deterred from making amends by fear of incurring injury to ourselves or causing injury to others. If we delay our amends merely out of fear for ourselves or others, we will ultimately be the ones to suffer. In these situations, we can seek outside guidance from a counselor or close friend to determine how to proceed. Otherwise, we will delay our growth, as well as experience stagnation in our progress toward building a new and healthier life.

- Which people on your amends list fall into this category? _____

_____

_____

_____

- Cite a situation in which making amends could cause serious problems. What are your options for making the amend? _____

_____

_____

_____

Situations which require deferred action.

Seeking another opinion could be helpful, when we have assessed that a particular amend might best be deferred. It is seldom wise to approach an individual who continues to suffer from our injustices. In situations where our own hurts are still deeply felt, waiting to make amends also might be wise. We know that amends must be made eventually, but timing is important so that we can benefit from the experience and not cause additional pain to ourselves or others.

- Which people on your amends list fall into this category? _____

_____

_____

_____

- Cite a situation in which you own hurts are causing a delay in amends-making. _____

_____

_____

_____

The process of making amends should not be confused with making apologies. When we apologize, we express regret for a fault or offense. An apology does not require action or imply a change in behavior. When we make an amend, we take action to improve, correct or alter that which we believe needs to be corrected. Apologies are sometimes appropriate, but apologies are not amends. We may discover, in apologizing, that we are using excessive explanation to excuse our behavior rather than simply change. We can apologize a hundred times for being late for work, but this will not "mend" our former tardiness. Appearing on time is a change in behavior, and thus becomes an amend.

- List two examples that indicate your ability to distinguish apologies from amends. _____

_____

_____

_____

Occasional emotional or spiritual relapses, or "slips," are to be expected and need to be dealt with in a compassionate and timely manner. When relapses occur, they are signals that we are probably hungry, angry, lonely or tired and are not being as vigilant as we might otherwise be. We may have even reclaimed control of our will from our Higher Power and need to go back to Step Three; or have eliminated something from our inventory and must return to Step Four; or have a character trait that we are not yet ready to relinquish and should repeat Step Six.

- Give examples of recent "slips" and how you dealt with them. _____

_____

_____

_____

- Which character traits caused the "slips?" What are your feelings about these slips? ____

_____

_____

_____

In reality, the Twelve Steps are intended to be repeated as we move toward our goal. Most of us need to repeat all or part of the Steps regularly, depending on our specific needs at a particular time throughout our course of recovery. After the first or second time through, we may not need to repeat the Steps in order. As we grow spiritually, we will be increasingly able to use them daily, as we journey toward further healing and a new life.

● What hesitancy do you experience in accepting the fact that working the Steps is a lifetime process? _____

_____

_____

_____

By repairing the damage we have done to others, we also will be overhauling our own lives. If we are thorough with our amends, we will find ourselves blessed with an amazingly peaceful state of mind, free of guilt and resentment. We may feel satisfaction in knowing that we have honestly done everything in our power to satisfy every material, moral and spiritual debt we have incurred—intentionally or unintentionally.

● What difficulty did you have performing Step Nine? How did you overcome it? _____

_____

_____

_____

The importance of Step Nine to our recovery process is obvious—it gives us a chance to put aside prior distractions and obsessions from our past, and to start living in the present. Since we have created and used this opportunity to repair past wrongs, we can now feel good about ourselves for our efforts to replace misery with serenity. The relief or joy we may give to others will never exceed the peace and increased self-esteem and acceptance this Step brings to us.

● In what ways are Step Five and Step Nine especially critical to your recovery? _____

_____

_____

_____

AMENDS GUIDELINES

The following is a summary of ideas and procedures that have been useful in preparing for and making the amends required in Step Nine.

Attitude

- Being willing to love and forgive yourself and the person to whom an amend is to be made.
- Knowing what you want to say and being careful not to blame the person with whom you are communicating.
- Taking responsibility for your part in the incident, what you are going to say and how you are going to say it.
- Being willing to accept the consequences.
- Resisting the desire for a specific response from the other person.
- Being willing to turn your anxieties over to God.

Preparation

- Devoting time to prayer and meditation.
- Delaying the amend if you are angry or upset and doing more Step Four inventory work.
- Keeping it simple. Details and explanations aren't necessary.
- Remembering that the amend does not focus on the other person's part in the situation.
- Expressing your desire or asking permission to make the amend. For example: *I am involved in a program that requires me to be aware of the harm I have done to others and to take responsibility for my actions. I'd like to make amends to you. Are you willing to receive them?*

Sample Amends

- *I was (scared, overwhelmed, feeling abandoned, etc.) when _____ happened between us. I ask your forgiveness for (harm done) and for anything else I may have done in the past by my thoughts, words or actions that caused you pain. It was not my intent to hurt you. Will you forgive me?*
- *I want to make an amend to you about _____ . For all those words that were said out of (fear, thoughtlessness, etc.) and confusion, I ask your forgiveness.*

AMENDS EXERCISE

Select a person to whom you wish to make an amend.

● Who is the person and what is the reason for the amend? _____

_____

_____

_____

_____

_____

● How will you communicate the amend? _____

_____

_____

_____

_____

_____

Write an amends letter to yourself.

● Dear _____ ,

_____

_____

_____

_____

_____

_____

_____

_____

_____

_____

_____

_____

● How do you feel as a result of writing this letter? _____

_____

_____

_____

_____

STEP TEN

Continued to take personal inventory and, when we were wrong, promptly admitted it.

❧

Our initial work with the Steps identifies the true nature of the ineffective and unhealthy behavior we have been using for most of our lives. We have examined our condition and made restitution for our misdeeds wherever possible. For many of us, the Steps may be our first antidote for relieving the pain created by our addictive behavior. Our commitment to continue working the Steps acknowledges our intention to improve the quality of our lives and relationships through reliance on our Higher Power.

● Which of your behaviors have been modified or eliminated since working the Steps? __

_____

_____

_____

● Which ineffective behaviors are still present? _____

_____

_____

_____

Step Ten initiates the maintenance phase of the Program. As it becomes apparent that spiritual growth is a lifelong process, we then understand that our progress must be maintained daily. When we accept the fact that healing can be achieved only one day at a time, the urgency to "finish the Program" diminishes.

● In what area do you feel most satisfied with your progress in the first Nine Steps? _____

_____

_____

_____

● In what area do you feel most dissatisfied with your progress in the first Nine Steps? __

_____

_____

_____

As we begin to feel better about ourselves and our lives, some of us may think we are "home free" and allow other activities to distract us or keep us from attending and participating in meetings. We may rationalize that we are too tired or have more important things to do. Some of us may even justify dropping out completely, in the belief that we are "cured." We may become irritable and short-tempered, not realizing that our recovery has been seriously jeopardized. If we continue on this course of self-deception, we may ultimately regress to an even greater degree of ineffectiveness.

- What is your current pattern of meeting attendance? _____

  _____

  _____

  _____

- How does your behavior indicate you are feeling "cured" and you no longer need to attend meetings regularly? Explain. _____

  _____

  _____

  _____

We should be alert to the danger signals (e.g. irritability, frustration, anxiety) that occur if we slip away from the philosophy of the Steps. New problems and confusions may be related to not fully accepting the Program, missing meetings, or losing our support system. If and when we decide to return to the meetings, we may find ourselves quickly revived by the warmth and enthusiasm that surrounds us. The emotional and spiritual uplift that meetings often inspire can encourage us to get back on the path with renewed effort. When the Twelve Step philosophy of life becomes an integral part of our daily activities, our attendance at meetings may decrease. Although we may not need to attend meetings regularly, we can be assured that they are there when we need them.

- What problems have arisen that you can attribute to missing meetings? _____

  _____

  _____

  _____

- What feelings are present that indicate you may need to attend more meetings? _____

  _____

  _____

  _____

Step Ten requires that we continue to take personal inventory and, when wrong, promptly admit it. This is a critical part of our recovery—we can no longer risk indulging in harmful attitudes and inappropriate behaviors. We must watch for signals that reactivate past resentments and fears or that suggest we are trying to manage our lives alone. When we see ineffective behaviors returning, we must stop ourselves and ask our Higher Power for help in removing them, then make amends promptly if harm has been done.

● What is the value of promptly admitting your wrongs? _____

_____

_____

_____

Our commitment to completing the remaining Steps requires that we fully acknowledge our need for continued and ongoing spiritual development. Just as our bodies tell us when to eat or sleep, our spiritual nature tells us when we need nourishment. We recognize that diligence in taking care of ourselves spiritually, emotionally and physically is necessary. As we begin to appreciate the idea that we are whole and complete, we are able to see the long-range possibilities for our future security. With the help of our Higher Power, we slowly become more able to "Let Go and Let God." As we learn to do this, our stress level greatly diminishes. The routine practice of Step Ten maintains our honesty and humility, and helps us to maintain our progress in recovery.

● Which activities and processes help you take care of yourself spiritually? _____

_____

_____

_____

The Program's emphasis on daily inventory is based on the realization that many of us haven't yet developed the tools necessary for self-appraisal. As we become more familiar and comfortable with personal inventories, we become more willing to invest the necessary time in exchange for the rewards received. Three types of inventories are recommended; each serves a different purpose. These are the **Spot-Check Inventory, Daily Inventory** and **Long-Term Periodic Inventory.**

● How will taking a daily inventory help you develop the ability to appraise your behavior?

_____

_____

_____

● How do you feel about taking a routine inventory? _____

_____

_____

_____

Spot-Check Inventory

This is a brief review of our thoughts, feelings and actions, done several times a day, as needed. It is a tool for examining each situation, seeing where we are wrong and taking prompt corrective action. Taking frequent inventories and promptly admitting our wrongs keeps us free from guilt and supports our spiritual growth.

- If you have not developed the daily habit of self-appraisal, how might you do so? _____

_____

_____

_____

In our daily activities, it is often hard to recognize that seemingly praiseworthy actions are, in fact, old behavior returning. For example, we may have a desire to do a favor for someone, and, in the process, we observe how considerate we are—how no one else would do what we are doing. Close examination of this behavior may indicate that we are still seeking approval and attempting to please others.

- List two examples of your "true" motives behind the "nice" things you do for others.

_____

_____

_____

Another tendency is to blame someone else for our wrong-doing. We may become righteously indignant and lose our tempers. We then try to justify our anger rather than take personal responsibility for our behavior. If we are sincerely working the Program, we will realize that our anger was not related to the other person's actions at all—it was a result of our own fears, anxieties and feelings of insecurity.

- Give examples of being angry at someone to cover up your own feelings. _____

_____

_____

_____

Daily Inventory

A review of the day's activities serves different and complementary purposes. It reminds us that this Program is lived one day at a time. It keeps us focused on today and prevents us from worrying about the future or living in the past. This inventory is much the same as our Step Four inventory, except we are concerned only with today. The review is brief and can be done just before going to sleep.

- How can you learn from daily inventories so that each day is an improvement on the day before? _____

_____

_____

_____

Situations may arise that challenge our integrity and commitment. In these cases, we need to be as honest and clear about our intentions as possible. Things to consider are:

- If we are slipping back, trying to control and manipulate others, we need to recognize it, take steps to correct it, then ask our Higher Power for help and guidance.

- If we are comparing ourselves to others and feeling inferior, we need to reach out to supportive friends and examine our feelings, in order to renew our own sense of self-acceptance.

- If we are becoming obsessive or compulsive and not taking care of ourselves, we need to stop and ask our Higher Power for help, not only in determining the unmet needs we are trying to fulfill, but also how to meet these needs.

- If we are fearing authority figures, we need to find the reason for our fear, acknowledge it, and ask our Higher Power for help in reacting appropriately.

- If we are depressed, we need to discover the central issue that is causing us to feel withdrawn or sorry for ourselves.

- If we are withholding our feelings, becoming uncommunicative or giving in to others' wants and needs, we need to take the necessary risks and express our feelings assertively.

- Which ineffective behaviors are most consistently present when taking your daily inventory? _____

_____

_____

_____

- What is your feeling about the presence of these behaviors? _____

_____

_____

_____

Long-Term Periodic Inventory

This is done once or twice a year and gives us a chance to reflect on our progress from a long-term perspective. Through this inventory, we will be able to see and celebrate the remarkable changes we have made in our lives. This is a time for humility and gratitude—a time to remember that our progress results from the spiritual growth we have attained through our partnership with our Higher Power. Long-term inventories also help us recognize problem areas and make necessary corrections. We may uncover previously undiscovered ineffective behavior as a result of our careful analysis.

- Which ineffective behaviors have surfaced as a result of your new experiences? _____

_____

_____

_____

Taking regular inventories proves invaluable as a means of keeping in touch with where we are and how we are behaving. It helps us determine if we are "on course" or slipping back into old behavior patterns. Being gentle and loving to ourselves and to our inner-child is a compassionate journey, made with a sincere desire to be restored to wholeness. Our Program is an individual one; it is reflected in how well we use the tools of the Program, namely the Twelve Steps. Our Higher Power is compassionate—watching lovingly as we falter and guiding us back on our feet when we ask for help. When an old behavior reappears or a new one is identified, we may want to keep the following points in mind:

■ When old behaviors reappear, they are simply repetitions of learned patterns of behavior. They reflect choices of our unconscious mind as it defended us against feelings of pain, strife, helplessness, guilt, revenge, disapproval, etc. Clinging to these patterns keeps us from achieving the spiritual growth we so desire.

■ We feel safe when something is familiar to us, even though it is a negative behavior pattern or addiction from the past that may ultimately cause us pain. We use it anyway, because it is familiar to us.

■ We victimize ourselves by allowing the past to occupy our thoughts. We can let go of the past by acknowledging the unmet responsibilities that created our struggle.

■ Releasing an old behavior pattern can be frightening. By surrendering it to our Higher Power, we learn to trust that we will receive the needed support to develop behaviors that are more appropriate for our present wants and needs.

■ We can reach out to loving and supportive friends. They are important ingredients in our recovery.

● How do you deal with old behaviors when they reappear? _____

_____

_____

_____

● In what areas are you slipping back into old behavior patterns? _____

_____

_____

_____

The ongoing practice of Step Ten has many benefits; most importantly, it strengthens and maintains our recovery. We find additional rewards in many areas, such as:

■ Relationship problems diminish. Taking inventory and admitting our wrongs promptly dissolves many misunderstandings without further incident.

■ We learn to express ourselves, rather than fear being "found out." We see that, by being honest, we do not need to hide behind a false front.

■ We no longer have to pretend we are flawless and, thus, can be candid about admitting our wrongs.

■ Through admitting our own wrongs, others may, in turn, become aware of the ineffectiveness of their own behavior. We develop a true understanding of others and become capable of intimacy.

● In which areas of your life are you experiencing the most benefits and rewards? _____

_____

_____

_____

● How do you feel about these new experiences? _____

_____

_____

_____

To effectively work Step Ten, we need to pay special attention to promptly admitting our wrongs. Delay in admitting them merely shows us how deeply ingrained some of our behavior patterns are. The sooner we are able to admit our wrongs, the sooner we can repair the harm done to ourselves and others. Vigilance in taking a daily inventory will help us develop a feeling of freedom, as we learn to promptly take care of things that bother us. Having taken an honest, in-depth look at ourselves, we are now ready to explore our relationship with our Higher Power and the community in Steps Eleven and Twelve.

● Write down your plan for making a daily review of your activities, so that you can promptly admit and correct your wrongs. _____

_____

_____

_____

Notes: _____

_____

_____

_____

_____

_____

_____

_____

_____

_____

_____

_____

_____

_____

_____

_____

STEP TEN DAILY INVENTORY LOG
Using the following ratings, record your level of functioning each day:
0 = Poor   1 = Fair   2 = Average   3 = Good   4 = Excellent

Characteristic (Limitation)	Mon.	Tue.	Wed.	Thur.	Fri.	Sat.	Sun.
Anger/resentment							
Approval seeking							
Caretaking							
Control							
Denial							
Depression/self-pity							
Dishonesty							
Frozen feelings							
Isolation							
Jealousy							
Perfectionism							
Procrastination							
Worry (past or future)							

Characteristic (Strength)	Mon.	Tues.	Wed.	Thur.	Fri.	Sat.	Sun.
Forgiveness							
Generosity							
Honesty							
Humility							
Patience							
Risk-taking							
Self-nurturing							
Tolerance							
Trust							

- What were your experiences in completing this exercise? _____

_____

_____

_____

- How did it help you be more aware of your behavior? _____

_____

_____

_____

STEP ELEVEN

Sought through prayer and meditation to improve our conscious contact with God as we understood God, praying only for knowledge of God's will for us and for the power to carry that out.

❧

Step Eleven is a means to deepen our partnership with our Higher Power. Having developed a relationship in Steps Two and Three, we have relied upon it heavily as we worked the subsequent Steps. In many cases, it was the single source of courage and strength for achieving our level of progress in the Program.

● As a result of your diligence in working the Steps, what has been revealed to you about your Higher Power's will for you? What are your feelings about this? _____

_____

_____

_____

At this point, we may have noticed that *"making a decision to turn our will and our lives over to the care of God"* is not a single event; it is a daily intention. Now we are being asked to *"pray for knowledge of God's will for us and for the power to carry that out."* We may find that seeking knowledge of God's will for us is an easier task than turning our will over, because of our previous persistent and repeated feelings of distrust in a Higher Power.

● How have you experienced the realization that "knowledge of God's will" comes to you only as a result of surrendering to your Higher Power? _____

_____

_____

_____

If we are periodically puzzled by the daily temptations and challenges we face, it may be because we are still Adult Children, learning to distinguish between "adult" and "childlike." Most of us are continually learning how to re-parent our fear-filled inner child. In his book "Your Inner Child of the Past," Dr. Missildine addresses our need to be aware of adult behavior that stems from damaging childhood experiences (e.g. temper tantrums, perfectionism, compulsive drinking or eating, careless spending and selfishness). We clearly are not doing God's will when we insist on living in a fantasy, ignoring our failures and pressing on in ever-widening circles of confusion.

● Identify ineffective behavior that indicates the presence of your fear-filled inner child. _

_____

_____

_____

- How does this behavior interfere with your relationship with God? _____
  _____
  _____
  _____

Our intention to do God's will can, at times, be compromised by the appearance of our old feelings and controlling attitudes. As we experience this struggle on a daily basis, the need for help from our Higher Power becomes more clear. In Step Eleven, we focus on deepening our relationship with our Higher Power. It is mostly through our quiet moments of prayer and meditation that the presence and guidance of a Higher Power becomes clear to us. As our relationship with our Higher Power improves, we see how we can rely and depend upon that Power for courage and strength in meeting life's challenges. We may experience a spiritual awakening that comes when we are willing and able to acknowledge, from the depth of our being, that a Higher Power can and will direct our lives.

- What is your understanding of God's will for you at this point in your life? How do you feel about it? _____
  _____
  _____
  _____

- Identify an important experience you have had with your Higher Power while working the Steps. Why was it important to you? _____
  _____
  _____
  _____

Step Eleven requires that we improve our conscious contact with God, as we understand God. To do this, we need to be consistent, patient and willing to practice. We have made contact with God in three of the earlier Steps. In Step Three, we made a decision to turn our will and our lives over to God's care. In Step Five, we admitted our wrongs directly to God. In Step Seven, we humbly asked God to help us remove our shortcomings. Step Eleven gives us a means of strengthening that contact and enables us to bring our Higher Power into our daily lives. Now we can let go of our feelings of aloneness and alienation and enjoy the quality partnership that is truly life-giving and life-sustaining.

- How has your relationship with your Higher Power improved since you began working the Steps? _____
  _____
  _____
  _____

● In what areas do you have difficulty asking for guidance from your Higher Power? _____

_____

_____

_____

The means suggested for improving our conscious contact with our Higher Power are prayer and meditation. These are two of the channels through which we reach God—and experience God's reach toward us. Prayer can mean focused thought, a talk directly with God or a request for guidance and knowledge of God's will in our affairs. Meditation is listening to God. Meditation techniques are designed to calm our minds and rid us of daily preoccupations and concerns, so we can hear God's guidance and will for our lives.

● What are your past experiences of prayer? _____

_____

_____

_____

● What are your past experiences of meditation? _____

_____

_____

_____

How do we pray, and for what do we pray? Many of us were taught to pray before we understood what it meant. In the beginning, we may have used the prayer *"Now I lay me down to sleep,..."* or asked God to bless Mommy and Daddy and others who were close to us. As we grew, our dysfunctional family experiences brought us great pain; those we depended upon hurt and disappointed us. Perhaps we blamed God for not hearing and answering our desperate prayers. Based on the Program's principles, our attitudes toward prayer change as we work the Steps. We learn to ask that God's will for our lives be shown to us, trusting that our best interests will be served. The old habit of praying for material things will diminish, to be replaced with prayers for guidance. We begin to rely upon some of the slogans and prayers, such as "Let Go and Let God" or The Serenity Prayer. Our prayers can be simple sentence prayers, such as *"God, please help me,"* or *"Thank you, Higher Power."* God will hear and respond to our most humble call for aid.

● List examples of what you pray for. How has the quality of your prayer changed? _____

_____

_____

_____

● How do you feel when praying to your Higher Power for help and guidance? _____

_____

_____

_____

Meditation is an ancient practice that involves the use of specific processes for calming the mind. During meditation, we establish a channel through which we can receive guidance from God. To meditate, we must quiet our conscious mind and remove the barriers established by our busy thoughts. This is difficult for some of us, because we are unaccustomed to sitting still and relaxing both body and mind. Meditation helps to calm us emotionally, relax us physically and release the unproductive energy we normally expend to keep our emotions and bodies in high gear.

●   In what ways has meditation revealed solutions that you could not have imagined? _____

_____

_____

_____

Methods of prayer and meditation may vary; however, it is our desire to hear and feel heard that matters. Our primary commitment is to deepen our relationship and expand our communication with our Higher Power. This means being honest about our feelings and thoughts, admitting our limitations and bringing our failings to God for forgiveness. Through a faithful and disciplined dedication to prayer and meditation, we become aware of God's unconditional love, forgiveness and constant presence in our lives. If we continue to pray with patience and trust, we will be rewarded with endless gifts of peace, serenity, love and joy.

●   In what ways has Step Eleven changed your practice of prayer and meditation? _____

_____

_____

_____

In our quest toward a spiritual awakening, Step Eleven provides us with a way to improve our conscious contact with God. In this Step, we pray *only for knowledge of God's will for us and for the power to carry that out.* Great benefits can be derived from this Step when we are able to ask for knowledge of God's will, then turn the outcome over to God. It takes courage to let go of the outcome and have patience to wait for the results.

●   What is your resistance to praying "only" for knowledge of your Higher Power's will and

for the power to carry that out? _____

_____

_____

_____

The miracle of this Step is that our past method of praying evolves into a form of meditation, whether or not we think we know how to meditate. Praying only for God's will and for the power to carry that out redirects our personal and worldly fixations and allows us to concentrate only on the will of our Higher Power. It empties our minds of our preoccupation with ourselves, making it possible to experience God's presence.

● How has practicing Step Eleven redirected your thoughts so that you can concentrate on the will of your Higher Power, rather than on your own will? _____

_____

_____

_____

If we place our will in God's care, and pray sincerely for guidance, we find ourselves trusting that our will is being redirected. We then experience the courage and power to act according to God's will for us. Seeking higher guidance is an experience in humility, because we are so accustomed to running our lives by our own plan and making demands on God to give us what we think we want. Our own desires and opinions are so much a part of us that we may, at times, view the will of a Higher Power as a manifestation of what we think should happen.

● Give examples that show you are not making demands of your Higher Power and are willing to let things work in God's time. _____

_____

_____

_____

We use prayer and meditation to improve our conscious contact with God as we understand God. As we work Step Eleven, we may see signs of progress, such as a deep sense of gratitude accompanied by a feeling of actually "belonging" in the world at last. We also may feel more secure as we develop a sense of being guided and sustained while we proceed with our activities. If we understand and follow the Program carefully, some of the changes in our lives will appear miraculous; others will be more gradual as we gain the skills we need to sustain our recovery.

● In what areas of your life do you experience a sense of gratitude? _____

_____

_____

_____

GUIDELINES FOR PRAYER AND MEDITATION

An overview of prayer and meditation for a given day may be outlined as follows:

At the beginning of the day, review your priorities and:
- Ask your Higher Power for direction in your thoughts and actions.
  - To keep you aware of self-pity, dishonesty or excessive self-interest.
  - To provide the guidance needed to take care of any problems.
- Ask your Higher Power for freedom from self-will.

During the day, in moments of indecision or fear:
- Ask your Higher Power for inspiration and guidance.
- Reflect on Step Three and turn it over.
  - Relax and breathe deeply several times.
  - Be aware of any desire to "be right."
- Pray to your Higher Power as often as necessary during the day.
  - "Higher Power, please help me remove this _____" (feeling, obsession, addiction, etc.).
- If possible, call a support person to identify and share what is happening.

At the end of the day, review the events that happened and:
- Reflect on Step Ten and take a personal inventory.
  - Ask your Higher Power for guidance in taking corrective action where necessary.
- Ask for knowledge of your Higher Power's will for you.
- Forgive yourself and ask your Higher Power to help you learn from your errors. This review is not intended to cause obsessive thinking, worry, remorse or morbid reflection.
- Give thanks to your Higher Power for the guidance and blessings that were part of the day.

JUST FOR TODAY

I will take a good look at myself and see that I have many addictive and compulsive traits that have become dominant in my life. I am at the mercy of these traits and unable to manage them. Seeing this, I admit that I need help.

I will acknowledge the presence of a Power greater than myself who has created me, is aware of all my needs and is fully capable of healing me and restoring me to a condition of clarity and stability. This power is God as I choose to understand God.

I will let go of the inclination to figure out my problems with my mind. No more analyzing…no more questioning. I now make a conscious decision to turn my life and my will over to the care and keeping of God. I surrender the thinking that tells me I must "run my own show" and make my own life happen. I am ready to be a transformed (changed) person, beginning now.

I will release the past, letting go of my guilt or regrets about what happened "back then." Finding fault or blaming myself and/or others keeps me stuck in the past.

I will forgive myself and others for the way we've been. I realize that our actions have arisen out of fear and insecurity. I now allow myself and others to "be." I no longer pass judgment on our lives, our chosen paths or our patterns of growth.

I will drop all anxiety about the future. I will live **this day** with as much joy, trust and serenity as I can, realizing that this day is all I can handle.

I will let go of my tendencies to be dependent on persons, possessions and patterns to fulfill me. I recognize that these things are only a temporary part of my existence and cannot provide the lasting security, inner peace or true freedom that I yearn to experience on a daily basis.

I will take responsibility for all aspects of my life: my choices, my feelings, my physical and mental health, my spiritual well-being, my paths of growth and the principles and values by which I live.

I will utilize all the energies within me that contribute to the betterment of my life and to the lives of others (e.g., expressing honesty, integrity and kindness). To all else, I firmly say, "No, thank you."

I will thank God for the opportunity to be set free from old attitudes and behavior patterns that prevent me from moving in the direction of my needed healing.

I will willingly share with others the wisdom, peace and strength I have received through this Program.

I will go forth into this day with enthusiasm, believing in my own value and worthiness, and with the determination to enjoy this day and give it my positive best, come what may.

JUST FOR TODAY EXERCISE

Review your expectations for today. Remember to ask for knowledge of God's will for you and for the power to carry that out.

- Just for today, I will _____

  _____

  _____

  _____

  _____

- Just for today, I will _____

  _____

  _____

  _____

  _____

- Just for today, I will _____

  _____

  _____

  _____

  _____

- Just for today, I will _____

  _____

  _____

  _____

  _____

- Just for today, I will _____

  _____

  _____

  _____

  _____

- Just for today, I will _____

  _____

  _____

  _____

  _____

STEP TWELVE

Having had a spiritual awakening as the result
of these steps, we tried to carry this message to others
and to practice these principles in all our affairs.

❧

The Twelfth Step is the goal we were seeking when we began our journey toward healing and recovery. As we worked our way through the Steps, personal intuition told us that there was hope for us when we completed the cycle of this process. No mystery surrounds the Twelve Steps when we realize that they really work for those who are willing to risk self-discovery through surrender to a Higher Power. If we have practiced the other eleven Steps to the best of our ability, we will receive all of the gifts that result from our surrendering to a Higher Power and can pass them on to others.

● List three ways in which the Twelve Steps have helped you to experience a new way of living. _____

_____

_____

_____

The process of working the Steps can be compared to the transformation of a caterpillar into a butterfly. The caterpillar does not understand that it will become a butterfly. All parts of the death of its former identity and its rebirth in the cocoon must be experienced to bring about the transformation. The story is told of a man who noticed a cocoon attached to a branch of a bush in his yard. As he started to pull it from the bush and throw it away, he noticed the end opening and a butterfly struggling to escape. In an effort to help the emerging butterfly, he carefully cut the cocoon apart. The butterfly feebly crawled from the opened cocoon and, within a few hours, died. It needed the strength it would have gained from its struggle for freedom to survive in the outside world. Similarly, our working the Steps is a process we must complete by ourselves. Any attempt by another person to do our work or find our answers for us would limit our ability to gain the emotional strength we need to function in a healthy manner.

● Explain your understanding of the butterfly story as it applies to your own struggle for freedom. _____

_____

_____

_____

If we use the awakening of our new state of consciousness and being, our spiritual relationship with God can be a gift. It is usually accompanied by a shift in our value system—where there was darkness, we now see light. For most of us, our awakening is subtle and can best be appreciated in hindsight. The maturity we gain by working the Steps enables us to view many past experiences, especially painful ones, as spiritual in nature. Our spiritual growth, therefore, can be viewed as the sum of these individual experiences. With each, we can identify the ways in which our Higher Power has guided us.

- Which spiritual experiences have been the most enlightening for you? _____
  _____
  _____
  _____

- How can you further enhance your spiritual understanding? _____
  _____
  _____
  _____

We become increasingly able to feel, do and believe what would not be possible had we relied solely on our own resources. We find that we possess honesty, humility, peace of mind and love to a degree we had never imagined. New values, based on an understanding of ourselves as children of God, give emotional and spiritual balance to our lives. With the help of our Higher Power, we continually discover new qualities and abilities in ourselves, as well as in those around us.

- In what ways do you experience yourself as a child of God, needing emotional and
  spiritual balance? _____
  _____
  _____
  _____

Spiritual growth is an ongoing process—it may have begun early in the Steps, but it will continue for the rest of our lives. Spiritual growth is not a distinct event with a clear beginning and ending; it is a continuing evolution of becoming more compassionate, loving, caring and content. Our relationships with our families improve as we draw closer, yet we recognize each other's need for independence. We rarely have unrealistic expectations of ourselves, and we accept others as they are, not as we might want them to be.

- Describe your current relationships with your family and friends? _____
  _____
  _____
  _____

- Describe your current feelings toward your family and friends. _____
_____
_____
_____

Because we know this Program works, and it is working for us, we are ready to share it with others. The message we carry to those who are in bondage, as we once were, is a liberating one. Sharing the message strengthens our own recovery and advances our spiritual growth. In return, the new strengths and insights we receive help us continue our growth in heart, mind and spirit. Our ability to effect change convinces others of the value of the Steps and, in this way, the Program grows and prospers.

- What is the recovery message you want to share with others? _____
_____
_____
_____

- In what way are you planning to do this (e.g., service work, lead meetings, start a Step Study)? _____
_____
_____
_____

There is no specific way to "carry this message to others" besides telling our stories as honestly as we can—by explaining what our lives were like, what happened to us as a result of the Steps and how our lives have changed. This is one time when truly being ourselves is the gift we give to others. It can happen anywhere—when we are called upon to do volunteer work, share in meetings, interact with co-workers and family members. Sharing our story with others often helps them recognize their own needs and teaches us more about humility and honesty. As we share our experience, strength and hope with newcomers, we can inspire them to solve their own problems, look at themselves honestly and stop blaming others for their pain.

- Describe a situation in which you have felt another person's life was impacted as a result of sharing your story. _____
_____
_____
_____

- What benefit did you receive as a result of this? _____
_____
_____
_____

Working with newcomers can be extremely rewarding, as it gives us a heightened appreciation of how far we have come, thanks to the Program. As we reflect on where we were when first introduced to the Program, we are filled with empathy for those who come to the Program feeling troubled, confused, resentful and seeking "instant relief." As they get to know us, they will descover that the decision to join is an individual one, made by most of us when we decided we had hurt and suffered enough and were willing to surrender.

Carrying the message to others may mean:

- Offering guidance and help to newcomers as they learn that the Program can be successful only through a commitment to do the work.

- Encouraging newcomers to be patient and gentle with themselves while working the Program one day at a time.

- Acknowledging to newcomers that revelations from working the Steps may be both painful and rewarding.

- Explain how carrying the message can be a gift to yourself and to your recovery. _____

_____

_____

_____

A recurring message throughout the Twelve Steps is the importance of humility and surrender to our Higher Power. As we *practice these principles in all our affairs,* the key factor in this process is our relationship with our Higher Power. Working closely with our Higher Power keeps us on the right course and helps us maintain our inner peace—a state we cannot achieve independently. It can only come to us when we admit powerlessness and are willing to work on our spiritual development, one day at a time.

- List the ways in which you rely upon your Higher Power. Give examples. _____

_____

_____

_____

Sometimes we become discouraged and lose sight of our progress. If this happens, we can compare our past behavior to our present and ask ourselves:

- Are we less isolated and no longer afraid of people in authority?

- Have we stopped seeking approval from others and accepted ourselves as we really are?

- Are we more selective in choosing those with whom we develop relationships, and more able to keep our own identity intact while in a relationship?

- Have we developed the ability to express our feelings?

- Have we stopped trying to dominate others?

- Are we no longer behaving childishly by turning friends or spouses into protective parents, or by being overly dependent?

- Are we paying attention to the needs of our inner child?

Affirmative answers indicate the extent of our progress toward a healthier and better way of living.

● Describe the progress you see in each of the above areas that result from completing this Twelve Step Workbook. _____

_____

_____

_____

As we practice our new behaviors in our daily affairs, life in general seems to be working better. For some of us, the new behaviors we use in family and work environments have a profoundly positive effect, and we see our loved ones embarking on the road to recovery in their own lives. This is truly a manifestation of our cooperation with our Higher Power. We can now see how the changes in our lives and our behavior can impact the lives of others.

● What changes do you see in important relationships that you can attribute to changes in your own behavior? _____

_____

_____

_____

A key to practicing the Program in all our affairs is using the Steps as an integral part of our lives. The discipline of taking a problem through all the Steps need not be a time-consuming process. Most of our confusion will we eliminated if we invite the unfailing support and guidance from our Higher Power. The end result leaves us with a sense of inner peace and increases our confidence in our ability to deal directly with each of our problems at any time.

● Having completed this workbook, what are you planning to do to continue "living" the Steps, one day at a time? _____

_____

_____

_____

The most confounding, yet the simplest, truth is that the Program is useful for *all* areas of our lives. All we need to do "in all our affairs" is to be willing to work the Steps and then "let go." The process is gradual, regenerative and never-ending. We slowly become more responsive to our Higher Power, and thus learn the meaning of love, growth, peace and serenity.

● What network of support have you established for yourself to remind you that, in carrying the message, actions speak louder than words? _____

_____

_____

_____

TWELVE STEP EXERCISE

- Identify a situation or condition in your life that is currently a source of resentment, fear, sadness, or anger. It may involve relationships (family, work, or personal), work environment, health or self-esteem. Write a brief statement describing the situation and indicating why it is a concern. _____

_____

_____

_____

Use the following exercise to apply the principles of the Twelve Steps to the above.

- **Step One:** In what ways are you powerless over this situation or condition, and how is it showing you the unmanageability of your life? _____

_____

_____

_____

- **Step Two:** How do you see your Higher Power as assisting you in being restored to wholeness? _____

_____

_____

_____

- **Step Three:** How does being willing to turn your life over to the care of God assist you in dealing with this? _____

_____

_____

_____

- **Step Four:** What character traits have surfaced (e.g., fear of abandonment or authority figures, control, approval seeking, obsessive/compulsive behavior, rescuing, taking inappropriate responsibility, not expressing feelings)? _____

_____

_____

_____

- **Step Five:** Admit your wrongs to God, to yourself and to another human being. _____

_____

_____

_____

- **Step Six:** Are you entirely ready to work in partnership with God to remove your ineffective behaviors? If not, explain. _____
_____
_____
_____

- **Step Seven:** Can you humbly ask God for help in removing your shortcomings? If not, what stands in your way? _____
_____
_____
_____

- **Step Eight:** Make a list of the persons harmed. _____
_____
_____
_____

- **Step Nine:** What amends are necessary, and how will you make them? _____
_____
_____
_____

- **Step Ten:** Review the above Steps to be sure that nothing has been overlooked. _____
_____
_____
_____

- **Step Eleven:** Take a moment for prayer or meditation, asking for knowledge of God's will for you. What did you discover? _____
_____
_____
_____

- **Step Twelve:** How can your understanding and spiritual guidance assist you in dealing with this problem? _____
_____
_____
_____

APPENDIX ONE

Methods of Study

There are two methods for using this workbook effectively: self-study and group study. Use this appendix as a guide to assist you in completing the workbook. The information contained in the self-study section also applies to group study.

Self-Study

Read the entire Step narrative for each Step before reading the questions. Then return to the beginning of the narrative and answer as many of the questions as you comfortably can. This will give you a better perspective of the overall scope of the material being presented. This material will not be graded for content or answering all of the questions. It is entirely for your benefit. Don't be discouraged if Steps One, Two and Three seem overwhelming to you—this is a common reaction for persons who are new to the Steps. Completion of these three Steps forms the foundation for working the Program.

As you proceed through the Steps, it is important to pace yourself. Work on each Step until you have completed as much as you can, and allow sufficient time to do the writing. This may take a day, a week or longer. Be patient with yourself; allow ample time to digest the content of each Step and reflect on its meaning. Impatience can seriously impair your effectiveness.

Depending upon how much of the material you complete, you may decide to go through the Step Study more than once. The Program is a lifelong process to be used in part or in whole on a daily basis. This workbook should not be your only involvement; it is just one part of working the Twelve Steps.

Wherever possible, share your insights with someone you trust. Communicating your discoveries to another human being can work miracles. In many Anonymous programs, this person is referred to as a sponsor. Sponsors are familiar with the Steps, and their insights and experiences can be invaluable, but be aware that your listener is not there to give advice or to heal you. The healing results from your relationship with your Higher Power.

If this workbook is your first exposure to the Twelve Steps and you are not presently participating in an Anonymous Twelve Step Program, it is important that you find a meeting to attend. The **Self-Help Resources** listed in this Appendix will help you identify the program for you. Other resources are also available. Check your library or the telephone directory under "social service organizations" or "crisis intervention."

Group Study

Once you have identified a Twelve Step Group with which you are comfortable, you can begin a committed Step-Study Writing Workshop. The following information will assist you in forming the workshop. Appendix Two includes **Sample Meeting Guidelines for Secretary** to assist the secretary in conducting the meeting. The focus of this information is on using the workbook. Additional reading material that can be included in the workshop is available from other sources. See Appendix Six for a list of suggested reading.

Starting a Step Study is not difficult. It involves making an announcement at one or more Anonymous meetings (Appendix One includes a **Sample Meeting Announcement).** Some people will attend only once or twice to examine the meeting and may decide not to return. It is suggested that the meeting be closed to newcomers in the third week. The workshop is designed to last twenty-eight weeks, in accordance with the Appendix Three weekly writing exercises.

Even though you start the workshop and may function as secretary, be sure to have a different leader each week. It is recommended that leadership rotate by "family group" rather than by individuals. This gives each "family group" an opportunity to provide leadership periodically. The meeting formats included in Appendix Two have proven to be effective, but they are suggestions only. Keep the format simple, so workshop participants can focus on working the Steps.

Previous workshops have revealed that trust develops most quickly in small "family groups" with a maximum of seven individuals. For example, if twenty-four people participate, it is recommended that the workshop be divided into four "family groups" with six members each. The "family groups" will congregate to complete the evening's writing exercise and to share within their group for a specified period. The final portion of the meeting is devoted to sharing in one all-inclusive group. There is no ideal arrangement, other than keeping the "family groups" small.

When people gather to work on material as challenging as the Steps, total agreement regarding the commitment to work is important. The **Participation Agreement** in Appendix Two, which is read and signed by each individual, supports this commitment.

During the workshop, various issues will surface. Perhaps dissension within the small groups will cause incompatibility. In many previous workshops, these issues were resolved without making changes within the group. The struggles within each family group were found to be reenactments of original family situations. Leaving the groups intact for the duration of the workshop allows participants to resolve their conflicts, fosters growth and strengthens the bonds within the family group.

As participants surrender to guidance from their Higher Power, many problems will be handled in a more constructive manner. As Adult Children, we are inclined to be caretakers, enablers and people-pleasers, indicated by our inability to confront inappropriate, hurtful or self-destructive behavior. Instead, we tend to be overly nice to each other. In keeping with the desire for a safe environment, excessive confrontation is usually not needed for the family group members to alter old patterns of behavior. However, straightforward feedback is critically important, with communication being limited to each one's personal experience in a given situation.

Due to our early exposure to negative behavior (e.g., resentment, greed, sexual abuse, dishonesty, gluttony, envy, laziness) and negative feelings (e.g., self-pity, sadness, insecurity, worry, fear of rejection, fear of abandonment), these patterns may seem normal to us. As we progress through the Steps, this habit of seeing negative behavior as normal can change. This material offers an opportunity to experience growth in many areas by increasing our feelings of self-worth and self-esteem. Therefore, positive feelings and thoughts need to be appreciated and encouraged. Take time during the workshop to ask for people's feelings about personal and group progress in the workshop. This enables the facilitator to encourage open, honest communication within the entire group and to air elements of discouragement or distress before they hinder the group's progress.

There is no "right" way to work the material. Each person has something to contribute in whatever way feels most comfortable. Results will be varied, but each participant will experience growth and change. If this is your first experience in a committed Step-Study Writing Workshop, you are encouraged to be in touch with individuals who are familiar with this material. Please feel free to contact us at (619) 275-1350 or write the publisher if you have any questions regarding the Step Study.

SELF-HELP RESOURCES

Adult Children of Alcoholics
Central Service Board
P.O. Box 3216
Torrance, California 90505
(213) 534-1815

Al-Anon/Alateen
Family Group Headquarters, Inc.
Madison Square Station
New York, New York 10010
(212) 683-1771

Alcoholics Anonymous
World Services, Inc.
468 Park Avenue
New York, New York 10016
(212) 686-1100

Co-Dependents Anonymous
P.O. Box 33577
Phoenix, Arizona 85067-3577
(602) 944-0141

Debtors Anonymous
P.O. Box 20322
New York, New York 10025-9992

Emotions Anonymous
P.O. Box 4245
St. Paul, Minnesota 55104

Gamblers Anonymous
P.O. Box 17173
Los Angeles, California 90017

Narcotics Anonymous
World Service Office
16155 Wyandotte Street
Van Nuys, California 91406
(818) 780-3951

National Association for
Children of Alcoholics
31706 Coast Highway, Suite 201
South Laguna, California 92677
(714) 499-3889

National Council on Alcoholism
12 West 21st Street
New York, New York 10010
(212) 206-6770

Overeaters Anonymous
World Service Office
2190 190th Street
Torrance, Californ ia 90504
(213) 320-7941

Sexaholics Anonymous
P.O. Box 300
Simi Valley, California 93062
(805) 581-3343

Are you Ready for the Next Step in Recovery?

A writing Step Study is starting using
The 12 Steps ... A Way Out

Beginning Date: _____

Day: _____

Time: _____

Location: _____

Step Study Writing Workshop Overview

Following is an outline of what to expect from participating in a Step Study Writing Workshop using the book **The 12 Steps—A Way Out** ($14.95).

- During the first three weeks, the meeting remains open so that anyone interested in experiencing the meeting format is welcomed to do so.

- After the third week, small family groups are formed. These groups are an important part of the Step Study process and encourage the development of trusting, supportive relationships during the weeks that follow.

- Beginning with the fourth week, the meeting is facilitated by each family group on a rotating basis. The meeting format is in Appendix Two of the workbook.

- Two weeks are devoted to completing most of the Steps.

- Read the workbook material and complete as much of the writing as possible in a timely manner.

- The writing exercise for each Step (Appendix Three), is the focus of the weekly meeting. Time is spent at the beginning of the meeting to complete the exercise, which then becomes the basis for family sharing.

- Remember that you are doing this work for your own personal growth. Set your own pace and accept your progress without having unrealistic expectations of yourself.

- This Program is worked most successfully **one day at a time.**

131

SAMPLE MEETING SCHEDULE

STEP STUDY WRITING WORKSHOP
THE 12 STEPS—A WAY OUT
PROGRAM SCHEDULE

WEEK	DATE	IN-CLASS EXERCISES	AT-HOME WORK
Intro Week 1	6/8	Overview or Workshop	Characteristics
Intro Week 2	6/15	Overview and Writing	Step One
Intro Week 3	6/29	Step 1 Week 1	Step One
4 (Closed)	7/6	Step 1 Week 2	Step Two
5	7/13	Step 2 Week 1	Step Two
6	7/20	Step 2 Week 2	Step Three
7	7/27	Step 3 Week 1	Step Three
8	8/3	Step 3 Week 2	Step Four
9	8/10	Step 4 Week 1	Step Four
10	8/17	Step 4 Week 2	Step Four
11	8/24	Step 4 Week 3	Step Five
12	8/31	Step 5 Week 1	Step Five
13	9/7	Step 5 Week 2	Get Current
14	9/14	*Special Program*	Step Six
15	9/21	Step 6 Week 1	Step Seven
16	9/28	Step 7 Week 1	Step Eight
17	10/5	Step 8 Week 1	Step Eight
18	10/12	Step 8 Week 2	Step Nine
19	10/19	Step 9 Week 1	Step Nine
20	10/26	Step 9 Week 2	Step Ten
21	11/2	Step 10 Week 1	Step Ten
22	11/9	Step 10 Week 2	Step Eleven
23	11/16	Step 11 Week 1	Step Eleven
24	11/23	Step 11 Week 2	Get Current
25	11/30	*Special Program*	Step Twelve
26	12/7	Step 12 Week 1	Step Twelve
27	12/14	Step 12 Week 2	
28	12/21	*Closing Meditation*	

The process of working the Steps can be compared to the transformation of a caterpillar into a butterfly. The caterpillar is not clear that it is going to be a butterfly. Each part of its death and rebirth in the cocoon must be experienced.

The story is told of a man who noticed a cocoon on a bush in his yard. As he started to remove it from the bush and throw it away, he noticed the end was opening and a butterfly was struggling to escape. In an effort to help the emerging butterfly, he took it inside and carefully cut the cocoon away with a razor blade. The butterfly feebly crawled away from the open cocoon and, within a few hours, died. It needed the strength it would have gained from the struggle to free itself in order to survive in the outside world.

Working the Steps is something that only we can do. Any attempt by another person to do our work or find answers for us inhibits our own recovery and limits our ability to become strong.

APPENDIX TWO

MILESTONES IN RECOVERY

Through working in partnership with our Higher Power and participating in the Twelve Step Program, we can look forward to achieving the following milestones in recovery.

- We feel comfortable with people, including authority figures.

- We have a strong identity and generally approve of ourselves.

- We accept and use personal criticism in a positive way.

- As we face our own life situation, we find we are attracted by strengths and understand the weaknesses in our relationships with other people.

- We are recovering through loving and focusing on ourselves; we accept responsibility for our own thoughts and actions.

- We feel comfortable standing up for ourselves when it is appropriate.

- We are enjoying peace and serenity, trusting that God is guiding our recovery.

- We love people who love and take care of themselves.

- We are free to feel and express our feelings even when they cause us pain.

- We have a healthy sense of self-esteem.

- We are developing new skills that allow us to initiate and complete ideas and projects.

- We take prudent action by first considering alternative behaviors and possible consequences.

- We rely more and more on our Higher Power.

THE TWELVE STEPS FOR ADULT CHILDREN

STEP ONE

We admitted we were powerless over the effects of addiction—that our lives had become unmanageable.

STEP TWO

Came to believe that a Power greater than ourselves could restore us to sanity.

STEP THREE

Made a decision to turn our will and our lives over to the care of God as we understood God.

STEP FOUR

Made a searching and fearless moral inventory of ourselves.

STEP FIVE

Admitted to God, to ourselves, and to another human being the exact nature of our wrongs.

STEP SIX

Were entirely ready to work in partnership with God to remove our ineffective behavior.

STEP SEVEN

Humbly asked God to help us remove our shortcomings.

STEP EIGHT

Made a list of all persons we had harmed and became willing to make amends to them all.

STEP NINE

Made direct amends to such people wherever possible, except when to do so would injure them or others.

STEP TEN

Continued to take personal inventory and, when we were wrong, promptly admitted it.

STEP ELEVEN

Sought through prayer and meditation to improve our conscious contact with God as we understood God, praying only for knowledge of God's will for us and for the power to carry that out.

STEP TWELVE

Having had a spiritual awakening as the result of these steps, we tried to carry this message to others, and to practice these principles in all our affairs.

SAMPLE STEP STUDY WRITING WORKSHOP PARTICIPATION AGREEMENT

I, _____ , agree to participate with my family in working the Twelve Steps and also agree to:

- Give my maximum effort by actively participating in weekly meetings and maintaining contact with my Step Study family between meetings.

- Be as confident as possible, relying on my Higher Power for help and healing.

- Support my family group by giving each person my undivided attention.

- Be as honest as possible in all things.

- Openly share my uncomfortable feelings when someone makes offensive comments or uses inappropriate language.

- Humbly submit to the process and do my best to suspend negative judgment.

- Schedule time between weekly meetings to complete the written work on the Step and to study the Step as thoroughly as possible.

- Accept the discomfort and unsettling behavior changes that may accompany working the Twelve Steps.

- Keep my commitment to myself and to my family group by regularly attending the weekly meetings.

- Share my experience, strength and hope during the meeting.

- Refrain from trying to "explain" situations when sharing, and do my best to clearly identify and share my feelings (e.g., joy, sadness, depression, anger, love, hate, guilt, loneliness, inadequacy).

- Incorporate the "Five Practices of Recovery" into my daily life by:
  - Attending meetings.
  - Working the Steps.
  - Praying and meditating daily.
  - Using the telephone to maintain contact with members of my family group.
  - Beginning and ending each day with the first three Steps.

COMMON FEELINGS AND BEHAVIORS OF ADULT CHILDREN

We have feelings of low self-esteem as a result of being criticized. We perpetuate these parental messages by judging ourselves and others harshly. We try to cover up our poor opinions of ourselves by being perfectionistic, controlling, contemptuous and gossipy.

We tend to isolate ourselves out of fear and to feel uneasy around other people, especially authority figures.

We are desperate for love and approval and will do anything to make people like us. Not wanting to hurt others, we remain "loyal" in situations and relationships even when evidence indicates our loyalty is undeserved.

We are intimidated by angry people and personal criticism. This causes us to feel inadequate and insecure.

We continue to attract emotionally unavailable people with addictive personalities.

We live life as victims, blaming others for our circumstances, and are attracted to other victims as friends and lovers. We confuse love with pity and tend to "love" people we can pity and rescue.

We are either super-responsible or super-irresponsible. We take responsibility for solving others' problems or expect others to be responsible for solving ours. This enables us to avoid being responsible for our own lives and choices.

We feel guilty when we stand up for ourselves or act in our own best interest. We give in to others' needs and opinions instead of taking care of ourselves.

We deny, minimize or repress our feelings as a result of our traumatic childhoods. We are unaware of the impact that our inability to identify and express our feelings has had on our adult lives.

We are dependent personalities who are so terrified of rejection or abandonment that we tend to stay in situations or relationships that are harmful to us. Our fears and dependency stop us from ending unfulfilling relationships and prevent us from entering into fulfilling ones.

Denial, repression, isolation, control, shame and inappropriate guilt are legacies from our family of origin. As a result of these symptoms, we feel hopeless and helpless.

We have difficulty with intimacy, security, trust and commitment in our relationships. Lacking clearly defined personal limits and boundaries, we become enmeshed in our partners' needs and emotions.

We tend to procrastinate and have difficulty following projects through from beginning to end.

We have a strong need to be in control. We over-react to change over which we have no control.

SAMPLE STEP STUDY WRITING WORKSHOP FORMAT
INTRODUCTORY MEETING—WEEK 1

Make copies of the following materials for the first three introductory meetings for those who do not have workbooks:

- *Step Study Writing Workshop Overview (page 131).*
- *Step One Narrative (pages 5-6).*
- *The Twelve Steps and Our Journey Toward Wholeness (page x).*
- *Common Feelings and Behaviors of Adult Children (pages 1-4).*
- *Participation Agreement (page 135).*
- *Week 2 Writing Exercise (page 155).*
- *Week 3 Writing Exercise (page 156).*

[REWARD PROMPTNESS BY STARTING THE MEETING ON TIME.]

7:00 [Allow approximately 25 minutes for the following.]

[All meetings begin with the following materials. Single copies of each are handed out to individuals to be read.]

[Pass out *Common Feelings and Behaviors of Adult Children, Milestones in Recovery* and *The Twelve Steps for Adult Children.*]

"Good evening! Welcome to the _____ Step Study Writing Workshop. My name is _____ , and I am an Adult Child. During my childhood, I was influenced by a dysfunctional family environment in which addictive, compulsive or obsessive behavior of an adult seriously damaged me. As a result, my own self-esteem was negatively affected. I recognize that dysfunctional behavior is generational, and it is my intention to stop it in my lifetime."

"It is possible to have the characteristics of an Adult Child without having biological parents who are, themselves, chemically dependent, outwardly abusive or violent. The characteristics could have been passed down by grandparents or significant others in our lives."

"As we begin our time together, please join me for a moment of silence, followed by the Serenity Prayer."

"I have asked _____ to read *Common Feelings and Behaviors of Adult Children.*"

"I have asked _____ to read *The Twelve Steps for Adult Children.*"

"I have asked _____ to read *Milestones in Recovery.*"

"Our tradition is to be self-supporting through our own monetary contributions. We ask for your contribution at this time to avoid interrupting the meeting."

[After the collection]:

"Please introduce yourself by giving your first name only. This respects the anonymity of those who are present. It is not a requirement that you disclose your identity."

[After the introduction]:

"I welcome each of you. A Step Study Writing Workshop is not easy. You will find that the writing we do on each of the Twelve Steps is a powerful healing tool. Working the Steps can be extremely difficult in the beginning stages of your recovery. We suggest you attend other meetings, open step study meetings and read additional materials relating to Adult Children. This will broaden your understanding and enhance your ability to participate in the Twelve Step process. One of the first lessons in recovery is to know your own limitations and participate only in those activities that support your recovery."

"During the first three weeks, you will have an opportunity to experience the process used in this workshop. You will be asked to make a decision about your personal commitment by the third meeting. The full Program requires twenty-eight weeks of work, study, reflection and growth."

"You will find new relationships opening up to you as you spend time with the group and share experiences, strengths and hopes. The quality of these relationships may be unlike any other you have experienced."

"The principal purpose of this workshop is to support healing and recovery. You will be asked to do some unfamiliar things, such as trusting others, practicing healthy dependence and interdependence, listening carefully and sharing your feelings. You will have the opportunity to experience what life within a healthy family can be."

7:25 [Allow approximately 30 minutes for the following.]

[Have copies of the *Step Study Writing Workshop Overview* available to distribute.]

[Read the *Step Study Writing Workshop Overview* aloud.]

"As the facilitator of this meeting, I will lead only the first three meetings. By the fourth meeting, "family groups" will have been formed, and each group will be responsible for leading the meeting on a rotating basis."

"This is an introductory meeting intended to provide an overview of the Step Study Writing Workshop using *The 12 Steps—A Way Out.*"

[Have copies of *Step One* narrative (first two pages) and *The Twelve Steps and Our Journey Toward Wholeness* available to distribute.]

"For those of you who have not purchased a copy of the workbook, I have a sample from *Step One* narrative and a copy of *The Twelve Steps and Our Journey Toward Wholeness.* For those who have the workbook, please turn to Step One, and we will review the format of the writing to be done between the weekly meetings."

[Select material from *Step One* narrative to be read aloud.]

"Before attempting to write responses to the questions relating to each Step, read the entire Step narrative for an overview of the material. Reading the Step narrative and responding to the questions prior to the meeting will significantly improve the value you will receive from participating in the Step Study."

[Select material from *The Twelve Steps and Our Journey Toward Wholeness* to be read aloud.]

"The Steps are a process that prepares you to allow a Higher Power, as you define that Higher Power, to transform behavior that is harmful to yourself and to others. Your willingness to commit to this workshop will help you experience changes in your behavior. Do not be too concerned with the writing. Do the best you can and work at your own pace. There are no right or wrong answers, and no right or wrong ways to complete the exercises."

"As the facilitator of the meeting, my purpose is to be your trusted servant. I will be working the Steps with you. Understand that I am here, as I believe you are, to share my experience, strength and hope."

"The principal commitment required to successfully complete this work is a willingness to engage in the process one day at a time, one meeting at a time. It is also vital to trust your Higher Power to take care of the outcome."

7:55 [Allow approximately 20 minutes for the following.]

"We will spend the next 20 minutes discussing what we just reviewed and *The Twelve Steps and Our Journey Toward Wholeness.*"

8:15 [Allow approximately 35 minutes for the following.]

[End of first discussion period]:

[Have copies of the *Week 2 Writing Exercise* available to distribute.]

"For those who do not have the workbook, I am going to distribute a sample of the *Week 2 Writing Exercise.*"

"Approximately ten minutes are allocated to the Writing Exercise during each Step Study meeting, followed by approximately forty-five minutes of family group sharing. The sharing is either about the evening's writing exercise or the writing in the workbook."

"Following the family group sharing, the meeting is open for discussion including all family groups. Approximately thirty minutes is spent on general sharing."

"The meeting lasts from 7:00 to 9:00: approximately two hours."

"At this time, the meeting is open for further discussion on miscellaneous questions relating to the workshop."

8:50 [Allow approximately 10 minutes to conclude the meeting.]

[End of group sharing]:

"The material used from the workbook each week will guide you through the writing processes dealing with each Step. It is not intended to provide all the possible information on each Step."

[Have a copy of *Common Feelings and Behaviors of Adult Children* available to distribute.]

"For the meeting next week, please read and respond to the questions from *Common Feelings and Behaviors of Adult Children.* Our writing and discussion will focus on this material."

[Ask for any announcements.]

"Reminder! What you hear at this meeting is confidential; leave it at this meeting! It is not for public disclosure or gossip. Please respect the privacy of those who shared with us tonight."

"Will everyone please clean up after themselves and help rearrange the room?"

"Will all who care to, please join me in the closing prayer?"

"9:00 [ADJOURN.]

SAMPLE STEP STUDY WRITING WORKSHOP FORMAT
INTRODUCTORY MEETING—WEEK 2

For those who do not have workbooks, this meeting will deal with the following materials:

- *Step Study Writing Workshop Overview (page 131).*
- *The Twelve Steps and Our Journey Toward Wholeness (page x).*
- *Common Feelings and Behaviors of Adult Children (pages 1-4).*
- *Week 2 Writing Exercise (page 155).*

[REWARD PROMPTNESS BY STARTING THE MEETING ON TIME.]

7:00 [Allow approximately 25 minutes for the following.]

[Pass out *Common Feelings and Behaviors of Adult Children, Milestones in Recovery* and *The Twelve Steps for Adult Children*.]

"Good evening! Welcome to the _____ *Step Study Writing Workshop.* My name is _____ , and I am an Adult Child. During my childhood, I was influenced by a dysfunctional family environment in which addictive, compulsive or obsessive behavior of an adult seriously damaged me. As a result, my own self-esteem was negatively affected. I recognize that dysfunctional behavior is generational, and it is my intention to stop it in my lifetime."

"It is possible to have the characteristics of an Adult Child without having biological parents who are, themselves, chemically dependent, outwardly abusive or violent. The characteristics could have been passed down by grandparents or significant others in our lives."

"As we begin our time together, please join me for a moment of silence, followed by the Serenity Prayer."

"I have asked _____ to read *Common Feelings and Behaviors of Adult Children.*"

"I have asked _____ to read *The Twelve Steps for Adult Children.*"

"I have asked _____ to read *Milestones in Recovery.*"

"Our tradition is to be self-supporting through our own monetary contributions. We ask for your contribution at this time to avoid interrupting the meeting."

[After the collection]:

"Please introduce yourself by giving your first name only. This respects the anonymity of those who are present. You are not required to disclose your identity."

[After the Introduction]:

[Pass out copies of *The Twelve Steps and Our Journey Toward Wholeness*].

"Those of you who were not here last week, please take a copy of this material. It contains an overview of the Twelve Steps and their application to your recovery program."

"I welcome each of you. A Step Study Writing Workshop is not easy. You will find that the writing we do on each of the Twelve Steps is a powerful healing tool. Working the Steps can be extremely difficult in the beginning stages of your recovery. We suggest you attend other meetings, open step-study meetings and read additional materials relating to Adult Children. This will broaden your understanding and enhance your ability to participate in the Twelve Step process. One of the first lessons in recovery is to know your own limitations and participate only in those activities that support your recovery."

"During this meeting and the one next week, you will have an opportunity to experience the process used in this workshop. You will be asked to make a decision about your personal commitment by next week. The full program requires twenty-eight weeks of work, study, reflection and growth."

"You will find new relationships opening up to you as you spend time with the group and share experiences, strengths and hopes. The quality of these relationships may be unlike any other you have experienced."

"The principal purpose of this workshop is to facilitate healing and recovery. You will be asked to do some unfamiliar things, such as trusting others, practicing healthy dependence and interdependence, listening carefully and sharing your feelings. You will have the opportunity to experience what life within a healthy family can be."

"If you decide to join this writing workshop, you will be asked to make the following commitments.

- Make a sincere effort to do the work, realizing that some of the material will cause personal discomfort.
  - Attend regularly (bring the body; the mind will follow).
  - Participate in the meeting and share to the best of your ability.
  - Take responsibility for doing what you need to do.
- Allow for change, exercising courage and patience. You don't have to do it all alone or all at once. Remember:
  - Choosing health will frequently be painful, will sometimes bring condemnation from others and will appear abnormal.
  - Participate in healthy family-type interaction.
  - Tell the truth and keep your word.
  - Be willing to accept support and to give it to others.
  - In this life, we can never be more or less than fallible human beings.
  - Identify and accept your limits and the limits of others—physically, mentally and emotionally.
- Accept the fact that this is a spiritual program, born of the realization that trust and reliance on our Higher Power is life-changing and life-affirming.
  - Recognize that healing is done by cooperating with our Higher Power.
  - Surrender to the fact that we are all equal recipients of the love of a Higher Power.
- Engage in "recovery-type" sharing as distinguished from "dumping."
  - Express "recovery-type" sharing, by communicating how your program is working to heal old patterns of addictive, compulsive or obsessive behavior.

• Avoid "dumping," which is stating your problems and looking at yourself as a victim, rather than as someone working a program of recovery."

7:25 [Allow approximately 10 minutes for the following.]

[Have copies of the *Step Study Writing Workshop Overview* available to distribute.]

[Read the *Step Study Writing Workshop Overview* and indicate in which week the meeting will be closed.]

7:35 [Allow approximately 15 minutes for the following.]

[Ask that small groups of four to six be formed, depending on the total group size.]

[Have copies of *Common Feelings and Behaviors of Adult Children* and *Week 2 writing exercise* available for those who do not have the workbook.]

"Before we start the writing exercise, please read along with me *Common Feelings and Behaviors of Adult Children.*"

[Prior to start of writing exercise]:

(If available, soft music is useful during writing segment.)

"Ten minutes are allowed to complete the individual writing process. I will give a two-minute warning to allow you to complete your writing."

7:50 [Allow approximately 25 minutes for the following.]

[End of writing time]:

"Sharing your writing work within each group will last twenty-five minutes. Focus on your writing and allow everyone to share. Until everyone has shared, please don't crosstalk. Crosstalk is when two people enter into a dialogue that excludes other group members. Please limit your comments or observations to your own personal experience. I'll give a three-minute warning to allow you to complete the sharing."

"Try not to intellectualize when sharing. To the best of your ability, share the feelings you experienced while writing (e.g., joy, sadness, anger, love, guilt, hurt, loneliness)."

8:15 [Allow approximately 35 minutes for the following.]

[End of small group sharing]:

"Please rearrange your chairs into one large circle. The meeting is now open for sharing tonight's experiences."

8:50 [Allow 10 minutes to conclude the meeting.]

[End of large group sharing]:

"The material used from the workbook each week will guide you through the writing processes dealing with each Step. It is not intended to provide all the possible information on each Step."

"Our discussion for next week will be based upon material from Step One. I recommend purchasing a copy of *The 12 Steps—A Way Out* if you plan to continue this workshop. Please read Step One and respond to the questions."

[Ask for any announcements.]

"Newcomers are invited to remain after the meeting to discuss any questions they may have about the Step Study."

"Reminder! What you hear at this meeting is confidential; please leave it at this meeting! It is not for public disclosure or gossip. Please respect the privacy of the persons who have shared here tonight."

"Will everyone please clean up after themselves and help rearrange the room?"

"Will all who care to, please join me in the closing prayer?"

9:00 [ADJOURN.]

SAMPLE STEP STUDY WRITING WORKSHOP FORMAT
INTRODUCTORY MEETING—WEEK 3

For those who do not have workbooks, this meeting will deal with the following materials:

- *Writing Step-Study Writing Workshop Overview (page 131).*
- *Participation Agreement (page 135).*
- *Week 3 Writing Exercise (page 156).*

[Have 3x5 cards available to be completed by participants. These will be used to form the family groups.]

[Reward promptness by starting the meeting on time.]

7:00 [Allow approximately 25 minutes for the following.]

[Pass out *Common Feelings and Behaviors of Adult Children*, *Milestones in Recovery* and *The Twelve Steps for Adult Children*.]

"Good evening! Welcome to the _____ Step Study Writing Workshop. My name is _____ , and I am an Adult Child. During my childhood, I was influenced by a dysfunctional family environment in which addictive, compulsive or obsessive behavior of an adult seriously damaged me. As a result, my own self-esteem was negatively affected. I recognize that dysfunctional behavior is generational, and it is my intention to stop it in my lifetime."

"It is possible to have the characteristics of an Adult Child without having biological parents who are, themselves, chemically dependent, outwardly abusive or violent. The characteristics could have been passed down by grandparents or significant others in our lives."

"As we begin our time together, please join me for a moment of silence, followed by the Serenity Prayer."

"I have asked _____ to read *Common Feelings and Behaviors of Adult Children.*"

"I have asked _____ to read *The Twelve Steps for Adult Children.*"

"I have asked _____ to read *Milestones in Recovery.*"

"Our tradition is to be self-supporting through our own monetary contributions. We ask for your contribution at this time to avoid interrupting the meeting."

[After the collection]:

"Please introduce yourself by giving your first name only. This respects the anonymity of those who are present. You are not required to disclose your identity."

[After the introductions]:

"I welcome each of you. A Step Study Writing Workshop is not easy. You will find that the writing we will do on each of the Twelve Steps is a powerful healing tool. Working the Steps can be extremely difficult at the beginning stages of your recovery. We suggest you attend other meetings, open step-study meetings and read additional materials relating to Adult Children. This will broaden your understanding and enhance your ability to participate in the Twelve Step process. One of the first lessons in recovery is to know your own limitations and participate only in those activities that support your recovery."

"This is the last open meeting where you will have an opportunity to experience the process used in this workshop. You will be asked to make a decision about your personal commitment at this meeting. The full Program requires twenty-eight weeks of work, study, reflection and growth. This is the third meeting; all subsequent meetings will be closed to newcomers."

"You will find new relationships opening up to you as you spend time with the group and share experiences, strengths and hopes. The quality of these relationships may be unlike any other you have experienced."

"The principal purpose of this workshop is to support healing and recovery. You will be asked to do some unfamiliar things, such as trusting others, practicing healthy dependence and interdependence, listening carefully and sharing your feelings. You will have the opportunity to experience what life within a healthy can be."

7:25 [Allow approximately 20 minutes for the following.]

"In a few minutes, I am going to pass out the *Participation Agreement.* This agreement establishes the guidelines we will use during this workshop. The effectiveness of this Program and the success of those individuals who preceded you form the basis for this agreement. Accepting them is your choice. The level of your success will depend upon your desire to be supportive to others working the Program and your willingness to abide by the agreement. Take the agreement with you this evening and bring it next week."

"Family groups are selected at random by dividing the name cards equally into groups. This is intended to be a method free from anyone's bias. This procedure may sound controlling, but it has been proven to be a safe and nonjudgmental approach to family group selection. It is a big step toward 'letting go'."

[Pass out 3x5 note cards and ask each individual to complete the card. These cards will be used to form family groups and create a group roster prior to the next meeting.]

"When completing the information on the cards, please note the following information:
- First name, last initial.
- Telephone numbers (day and evening and the best time to call).
- Group preference (women only, men only or mixed). This has been included for the benefit of those individuals who feel that this will support their participation.
- Friends or relatives participating in this workshop with you. It works best if friends and relatives are not in the same group.

[Ask for small groups of four to six people to be formed, depending upon the total group size.]

[Refer to *Participation Agreement* in Appendix Two.]

[Read the *Participation Agreement,* using the *Facilitator's Script* in Appendix Two as a guideline.]

[Have a copy of the *Participation Agreement* and *Week 3 Writing Exercise* available for those who do not have the workbook.]

7:45 [Allow approximately 10 minutes for writing.]

[Prior to start of writing exercise]:

(If available, soft music is useful during writing segment.)

"Ten minutes are allowed to complete the individual writing process. I will give a three-minute warning to allow you to complete your writing."

7:55 [Allow approximately 25 minutes for the following.]

[End of writing time]:

"Sharing your writing work within each group will last twenty-five minutes. Focus on your writing and allow everyone to share. Until everyone has shared, please don't crosstalk. Cross-talk is when two people enter into a dialogue that excludes other group members. Please limit your comments or observations to your own personal experience. I'll give a three-minute warning to allow you to complete the sharing."

"Try not to intellectualize when sharing. To the best of your ability, share the feelings you experienced while writing (e.g., joy, sadness, anger, love, guilt, hurt, loneliness)."

8:20 [Allow approximately 30 minutes for the following.]

[End of small group sharing]:

"Please rearrange your chairs into one large circle. The meeting is now open for sharing tonight's experiences."

8:50 [Allow 10 minutes to conclude the meeting.]

[End of large group sharing]:

"If you plan to continue this workshop, please purchase a copy of ***The 12 Steps—A Way Out*** and begin reading and responding to the questions in Step One."

"The material used from the workbook each week will guide you through the writing processes dealing with each Step. It is not intended to provide all the possible information on each Step."

[Ask for any announcements.]

"Reminder! What you hear at this meeting is confidential; please leave it at this meeting! It is not for public disclosure or gossip. Please respect the privacy of those who shared here tonight."

"Will everyone please clean up after themselves and help rearrange the room?"

"Will all who care to, please join me in the closing prayer?"

9:00 [ADJOURN.]

MEETING PREPARATION FOR WEEK 4

- Assign family groups by sorting the 3x5 cards randomly into family groups. Use any method that is free of bias.

- Prepare a group roster of all participants, divided into family groups. The list is to include first name, last initial and telephone number.

- Have copies of the group roster available to distribute.

- If possible, participants who have indicated a desire to be in an exclusively female or male group should be in one group.

FACILITATOR'S SCRIPT

STEP STUDY WRITING WORKSHOP PARTICIPATION AGREEMENT

Secretary: When discussing the **Participation Agreement,** it is helpful to use this work sheet in order to expand the explanation and emphasize the value of the **Participation Agreement.**

Give my maximum effort by actively participating in weekly meetings and maintaining contact with my Step Study family members between meetings.

- Steps One, Two and Three are the foundation Steps.
  - They build inner strength and encourage the development of our capacity to rely on our relationship with our Higher Power.
  - Violation of Steps Two and Three is often the basis for further trouble and confusion.
- In choosing health and recovery, we must be prepared to discover that:
  - Our journey frequently can be painful as a result of changes that take place.
  - Our new patterns and habits may frequently bring condemnation from others who are confounded by our changed behavior.
  - Electing to seek a new life may appear abnormal, since our pre-recovery behavior has been seen as "normal" by us and many people around us.

Be as confident as possible, relying on my Higher Power for help and healing.

- We are all equal recipients of the love of a Higher Power as we understand and experience that Power.
- We will acknowledge our humanity by working Step One to the utmost of our ability. Remember, only through our cooperating with our Higher Power does the healing take place. To be available for healing we need to:
  - Work the Steps consistently.
  - Meditate and pray for healing, recovery and miracles.
- Our intention in this workshop is to develop skills and relationships that will enhance our ability to:
  - Nurture and be a loving parent to ourselves.
  - Create a network of support for ourselves and others. Support my family group by giving each person my undivided attention.

- To support each other in nurturing and healing we must:
  - Not interrupt.
  - Be genuinely there. We give support through example.
  - Realize that we each have a Higher Power relationship that works through us to enable us to break through barriers.
  - Suspend judgment or evaluation of progress.
  - Not support others when they choose to ignore or refuse to deal with their problems.

Be as honest as possible in all things.
  - Telling the truth, as we know it, may be a new experience for us.
  - Denial is confronted when we are honest with others and ourselves.

Openly share my uncomfortable feelings when someone makes offensive comments or uses inappropriate language.
  - By honestly acknowledging how we experience another person's communication, we respect our individual needs.
    - We do not have to accept verbal abuse.
    - We do not have to remain in the presence of anyone who is using language that offends us.

Humbly submit to the process and do my best to suspend negative judgment.
  - Regardless of how we feel, do as much of the work as is possible.
  - The format of this workshop includes structure and writing as regular parts of the process. The procedures used are directly related to the purpose intended.
  - The major differences between this workshop and other Twelve Step groups are:
    - The commitment to write; this is a critically important part of the workshop. It is important to follow the directions whether or not we agree with them.
    - The lack of focus on emotional support alone. If this is the only need, other options are available, such as seeing a trained counselor or therapist.

Schedule time between weekly meetings to complete the written work on the Step and to study the Step as thoroughly as possible.
  - Having family group meetings before the regular workshop time may allow for interaction that the workshop does not provide. Each family group will have to assess the need for this as they get to know each other.
  - Greater understanding of the healing process can be gained by studying material on the Twelve Steps, co-dependency and self-parenting. See Appendix Six for a partial list of appropriate supplemental materials.

Accept the discomfort and unsettling behavior changes that may accompany working the Twelve Steps.
  - Avoid the common mistake made during the process of recovery: that is, resorting to addictive, compulsive or obsessive behavior to distract from the pain.

- To make the greatest progress in working the Steps, it is best to refrain from developing a new intimate or sexual relationship with anyone. Such a focus can detract from our commitment to recovery from co-dependent relationships.

- Friendships can and will develop from this Program. Rely on these new relationships for support in experiencing the utmost from the Step work.

Keep my commitment to myself and to my family group by regularly attending the weekly meetings.

- Schedule other activities around meetings.

- Only an emergency is a bona-fide excuse for nonattendance.

- Harmony and results in this Step Study will be enhanced if family group members interact and communicate with one another between meetings.

Share my experience, strength and hope during the meeting.

- We demonstrate support by:

  • Not giving advice.

  • Taking responsibility for ourselves, rather than trying to fix others.

  • Being honest.

  • Withholding judgment. It is not helpful to point out what's wrong with another person's behavior.

- People will get what they need either in the meeting or in their daily lives; we are not responsible for providing their needs.

Refrain from trying to "explain" situations when sharing, and do my best to clearly identify and share my feelings (e.g., joy, sadness depression, anger, love, hate, guilt, loneliness, inadequacy).

- Feelings do not require analysis; they are emotions, pleasurable or unpleasurable, that one may have to a given situation.

- Pay attention to what our bodies are saying. Many of us cannot distinguish one sensation from another. As we progress in this work, appropriate labels for feelings will develop.

Incorporate the "Five Practices of Recovery" into my daily life.

- We learn from others, and others learn from us. The most useful arena for sharing recovery experiences is the step study meeting.

- Reading about the Steps fosters understanding; doing the required work in each Step assures results.

- Our Higher Power is always available and patiently waits for us to pray and meditate daily.

- The most immediate way to request support when we need it is to use the telephone. Often, a spontaneous call is an opportunity to acknowledge that we are thinking of someone and appreciate his or her presence in our lives. The telephone works both ways.

- All evidence indicates that we will be confronted daily by our human nature. Our relationship with our Higher Power is strengthened when we can begin and end each day with a review of our work in the first three Steps.

SAMPLE STEP STUDY WRITING WORKSHOP FORMAT
WEEK 4 TO WEEK 28

[Reward promptness by starting the meeting on time.]

7:00 [Allow approximately 15 minutes for the following.]

[Pass out *Milestones in Recovery* and *The Twelve Steps for Adult Children*.]

"Will everyone please be seated with their family groups."

"Good evening! Welcome to the _____ Step Study Writing Workshop. My name is _____ , and I am your trusted servant for tonight."

"Please join me for a moment of silence, after which we will recite the Serenity Prayer."

"I have asked _____ to read *Milestones in Recovery.*"

"I have asked to read *The Twelve Steps for Adult Children.*"

"Our tradition is to be self-supporting through our own contributions. We ask for your contribution at this time to avoid interrupting the meeting."

7:15 [Allow approximately 10 minutes for writing.]

[Prior to start of writing exercise]:

(If available, soft music is useful during writing segment.)

"Ten minutes are allowed to complete for writing, followed by forty-five minutes of family sharing. Then we will all join together."

"The writing and sharing topic for tonight is on Step _____ . Focus on your writing and allow time for everyone to share. Until everyone has shared, please do not crosstalk. Crosstalk is when two people enter into a dialogue that excludes other group members. Your sharing is most valuable when you limit your comments or observations to your own personal experience. I'll give a three-minute warning to complete the sharing."

[Start music if available.]

[Give a three-minute warning prior to the end of family writing.]

7:25 [Allow 45 minutes for family group sharing.]

[Give a three-minute warning prior to the end of family sharing.]

8:10 [Allow 5 minutes to form the large group.]

[Stop music; announce that it is time to form the large group.]

"Please open the family groups to include everyone."

[When everyone is seated]:

8:15: [Allow 30 minutes for large group sharing.]

"Will everyone please introduce themselves by giving their first names."

"During the remaining thirty minutes, please limit your sharing to three minutes so that everyone has an opportunity to share. To begin the sharing, does someone have a recovery experience from working the Steps or results from family group interaction during the previous week?"

8:45 [Allow 10 minutes for the following.]

"Are there any announcements?"

8:55 [Optional.]

"I have asked _____ to read the *Participation Agreement.*"

[See *Workshop Schedule* to announce the group leading next week.]

"Family group number _____ is leading the meeting next week."

"Reminder! What you hear at this meeting is confidential; please leave it at this meeting! It is not for public disclosure or gossip. Please respect the privacy of those who shared here tonight."

"Will everyone please clean up after themselves and help rearrange the room?"

"Will all who care to, please join me in the closing prayer?"

"Keep coming back, it works!"

9:00 [ADJOURN.]

SAMPLE MEETING GUIDELINES FOR MEETING SECRETARY

These guidelines are to be used by the secretary or the person who is leading the meeting for the evening.

- Before the regular meeting begins, read through the evening's writing exercise that includes material on the Step.
- Ask each group to phone those who are absent in order to support their next attendance.
- Remind the groups to focus individual sharing on the Step being worked. Encourage recovery-type sharing.
  - Sharing is to be focused on individual experience, strength and hope in working the Steps.
  - It is not necessary for everyone to share.
  - Allow equal time for everyone in the group to share.
- Encourage each group to meet at another time for more opportunities to process writing and to deepen family group bonding and trust. An alternative to meeting is telephoning regularly. See Appendix Five for a telephone roster.
- Encourage group members to share outside reading. Emphasize the importance of doing outside reading to broaden one's understanding of the Steps.
- Be as loving, supportive and positive as possible, recognizing you won't always feel this way.
- Be a good friend who is willing to listen, yet does not give advice.

APPENDIX THREE

FAMILY GROUP COMMUNICATION, SUPPORT AND RECOVERY

Quality communication among family group members is essential for successful completion of the materials in the step narrative portion and weekly writing exercises. Before you read any further, please take a moment to review what was written about the family group experiences in the **Methods of Study** in Appendix One.

The **Step Study Writing Workshop** is a method for looking at painful experiences from our past that are continuing to influence our lives today. Writing about and sharing our progress with the Steps involves a process of re-defining our knowledge and understanding of ourselves. As we share our recovery story with our family group, we will discover how our attitudes about ourselves and others are often founded on faulty information. Information has been passed on to us from parents, siblings and other relatives who did not know, or perhaps care to know, the truth about their own worth and value, or the beauty of other people.

As we work through the material in this Step Study, we will begin to see life through the eyes of an adult, rather than the eyes of a terrified, fearful and shame-filled child. We are not in this program to continue to view ourselves as victims. We are here to accept the reality of the past and work to enhance the quality of our present lives through working the Twelve Steps.

We will be sharing the process of our recovery with our family group members. Supporting one another in identifying the fears and resentments of our past will help us break the vicious cycle of passing dysfunctional and addictive behavior on to our own children. If we are not restored to wholeness, our own children may also be faced with maladaptive behavior in their lives.

A challenge often faced by participants working this material is developing a desire and a means to communicate with family group members between weekly meetings. This is an important factor in successful working of the materials in this book. We may be unaccustomed to having people actively interested in improving the quality of our lives. Sharing with family group members offers an opportunity to experience supportive-type relating. Sharing in the weekly meetings and being in contact with family members between meetings is a way to discover new "friends in recovery."

Successful sharing begins with the realization that the members of our family group cannot read our minds. If we find ourselves becoming resentful or angry because others are not responding to our problems, we need to remember that they cannot know or respond to what we don't tell them. If we are reluctant to share because our confidences have been betrayed in the past, this is an opportunity to rebuild our trust. By sharing openly we discover what is in our own hearts and minds. The dynamics of self-revelation (discovering exactly what we feel and think) occur through communicating with other persons. Through the process of sharing, something mysterious, powerful and subtle happens that gives us the courage to shed our fear of discovery. By asking for and receiving the support of others, we are empowered to allow the past to slip away and to develop a new life.

As we write and share the working of this material, our stories may be ones we have told in the past. It is important to view our sharing as re-defining our past behavior, not telling and re-telling the unhappy details of shattered dreams and painful childhood experiences. If our stories are repeated often and dramatically, we may find them being exaggerated as they are retold. We must examine our motives for re-telling the drama of our past. Is it because we feel like victims? Are we blaming others or making excuses? Are we wallowing in our past miseries and re-charging old resentments? Part of our recovery is getting rid of our old behavior. This means taking time to listen carefully to what we are sharing and asking the family group members to respond to our communication. If what we are talking about does not support our recovery, there is no reason for sharing it.

Some of us have never overcome the fear of revealing our true feelings. We justify this fear by stating that we have nothing to offer. This is not true, and since the quality of our relationships will be determined by the honesty of our sharing, we *must* each learn how to open ourselves to others in our family group. This process will post another milestone in the task of breaking the destructive cycle of failure feeding upon failure. By sharing openly, we demonstrate that we trust our family group and willingly agree to be vulnerable to them. Nothing equals the importance of revealing our real selves so we can be known, healed and loved.

This work also prepares us to become mentors to other people who are newly aware of themselves as Adult Children. In this workshop and in other places and times, we demonstrate to others what we are learning for ourselves. We all take turns being followers until we are ready to lead. Those who preceded us enabled us to follow their example as they shared their experience, strength and hope. We learn from others by the principles and practices that produced positive and healthy experiences for them. By our continued commitment to heal our ineffective behavior, we will find others looking to us for comfort, direction and wisdom.

For many of us, our participation in this Step Study makes us want to bring together members of our biological families who may be estranged from us or each other. This is because each of us has a deep desire to participate as loved and loving members of a healthy and whole family system. We may be able to do this with our own families, or we may discover that our real family is made up of people who love us, whether they are relatives or not. During holidays and other family-type celebrations, there will be ample opportunities for us to choose to enjoy the occasion with our "new" family members. We have the choice to connect with either or both families of loved ones who welcome our participation with them. This is clearly a time for us to realize that in our program of recovery, we no longer have to be without a loving family.

COMMON FEELINGS AND BEHAVIORS
PROCESSES AND QUESTIONS FOR WEEK 2

- Refer to **Common Feelings and Behaviors of Adult Children** (page 1.) Select the feeling or behavior that best describes you in a given situation and indicate how it is currently affecting your life. _____

  _____

  _____

  _____

  _____

  _____

  _____

- What changes would you like to see in your life as a result of working the Steps? _____

  _____

  _____

  _____

  _____

  _____

  _____

  _____

- What questions or resistance do you have regarding the format of this workshop? _____

  _____

  _____

  _____

  _____

  _____

  _____

Allocate equal time for each family member. Please limit individual sharing to feelings and explanations of the written material. Allow time for contributions from family members after writing has been shared.

WORKSHOP PARTICIPATION AGREEMENT
PROCESSES AND QUESTIONS FOR WEEK 3

● What is your main objective in choosing to participate in this workshop? _____

_____

_____

_____

_____

_____

● What anxieties do you feel about making a weekly commitment for a six-month period? __

_____

_____

_____

_____

_____

_____

● Which parts of the **Participation Agreement** do you feel positive about and can easily

support? _____

_____

_____

_____

_____

_____

● Which part of the **Participation Agreement** do you feel negative about and cannot easily

support? _____

_____

_____

_____

_____

_____

Allocate equal time for each family member. Please limit individual sharing to feelings and expla-nations of the written material. Allow time for contributions from family members after writing has been shared.

STEP ONE
PROCESSES AND QUESTIONS FOR WEEK 4 (Step 1—Week 1)

We admitted we were powerless over the effects of addiction—
that our lives had become unmanageable.

● As part of tonight's family group sharing, introduce yourself and share a brief story about your background. Also, restate for your family group your main objective in choosing to participate in this workshop. (See Week 3 Writing Exercise.) _____

_____

_____

_____

_____

_____

_____

_____

● Accepting the notion that you have the power to make choices in your life, where do you feel "powerless" because one of your choices is not going the way you want it? _____

_____

_____

_____

_____

_____

_____

_____

_____

_____

_____

_____

_____

_____

Allocate equal time for each family member. Please limit individual sharing to feelings and explanations of the written material. Allow time for contributions from family members after writing has been shared.

FAMILY GROUP CONTACT RECORD
WEEK 5

Date: _____ Person _____ Subject _____

Result of communication and action taken: _____

_____

_____

_____

Feelings experienced (love, anger, pain, support, acknowledgement): _____

_____

_____

_____

Date: _____ Person _____ Subject _____

Result of communication and action taken: _____

_____

_____

_____

Feelings experienced (love, anger, pain, support, acknowledgement): _____

_____

_____

_____

Summary of Week's events: _____

_____

_____

_____

_____

_____

_____

_____

_____

_____

Week 6 Writing Exercise focuses on *Family Group Communication, Support and Recovery.*

STEP ONE
PROCESSES AND QUESTIONS FOR WEEK 5 (Step 1—Week 2)

We admitted we were powerless over the effects of addiction—
that our lives had become unmanageable.

● List events that occurred during the week that illustrate your feelings of powerlessness.

_____

_____

_____

_____

_____

● List events that occurred during the week that illustrate the unmanageable situations in your life. _____

_____

_____

_____

_____

_____

● Explain how the experiences described in the above questions are reenactments of the dysfunction in your childhood. _____

_____

_____

_____

_____

● What difficulties do you have in revealing yourself to others? _____

_____

_____

_____

_____

_____

Allocate equal time for each family member. Please limit individual sharing to feelings and expla-
nations of the written material. Allow time for contributions from family members after writing
has been shared.

FAMILY GROUP CONTACT RECORD
WEEK 6

Date: _____ Person _____ Subject _____

Result of communication and action taken: _____

_____

_____

_____

Feelings experienced (love, anger, pain, support, acknowledgement): _____

_____

_____

_____

Summary of Week's events: _____

_____

_____

_____

_____

_____

_____

A WORD ABOUT LEAVING YOUR FAMILY GROUP

Most of us are free to do as we please. When we want to go, we go; when we want to stay, we stay. Participating with your family group has possibly raised some questions as to the compatibility of your family members and made you feel like you didn't want to stay with your family. If you are experiencing pain, frustration or discomfort from working the Step material, you may feel discouraged and fearful. You may have fallen behind, and are finding it difficult to complete the work. If you have not developed a close bond with your family members, you may consider quitting.

If any of these feelings and thoughts are present, we strongly suggest that you:

■ Take a risk; reach out to your family group (or an individual member), and share your true feelings and fears.

■ Take time to consider the options; ask for help from the Lord, and make the decision which will be best for you.

When you make your final decision, inform your family members. Allow them to preserve the dignity of their experience. Do not be concerned about their reaction. It is important for you to become able to express your needs and wants, and realize that other people are there to be supportive. This is a healthy way to complete the relationship, and will help to minimize any feelings of abandonment which may result from your decision to leave.

STEP TWO
PROCESSES AND QUESTIONS FOR WEEK 6 (Step 2—Week 1)

*Came to believe that a Power greater than ourselves
could restore us to wholeness.*

- What difficulties are you having in accepting a Higher Power? Identify any childhood memories that may be getting in your way. _____
  _____
  _____
  _____
  _____
  _____
  _____

- What events occurred during the week that demonstrate your ineffective behavior? How do you feel right now about this experience? _____
  _____
  _____
  _____
  _____
  _____
  _____

- The **Introduction to Family Group Communication, Support and Recovery** (page 153) emphasizes the importance of contact with your family group outside the regular meeting. What arrangements can you now make to initiate regular contact (e.g. arrange for phone calls or meeting during the week)? What feelings do you have about this commitment that you want to express tonight? _____
  _____
  _____
  _____
  _____
  _____
  _____

Allocate equal time for each family member. Please limit individual sharing to feelings and explanations of the written material. Allow time for contributions from family members after writing has been shared.

FAMILY GROUP CONTACT RECORD
WEEK 7

Date: _____ Person _____ Subject _____

Result of communication and action taken: _____

_____

_____

_____

Feelings experienced (love, anger, pain, support, acknowledgement): _____

_____

_____

_____

Date: _____ Person _____ Subject _____

Result of communication and action taken: _____

_____

_____

_____

Feelings experienced (love, anger, pain, support, acknowledgement): _____

_____

_____

_____

Summary of Week's events: _____

_____

_____

_____

_____

_____

_____

_____

_____

_____

_____

_____

STEP TWO
PROCESSES AND QUESTIONS FOR WEEK 7 (Step 2—Week 2)

*Came to believe that a Power greater than ourselves
could restore us to wholeness.*

- Describe your relationship with God during childhood, as well as your current feelings about that relationship. _____

  _____

  _____

  _____

  _____

  _____

- What events in your life interfere with your relationship with a Higher Power? _____

  _____

  _____

  _____

  _____

  _____

- What difficulties do you have in accepting that your Higher Power can restore you to wholeness? _____

  _____

  _____

  _____

  _____

  _____

- What strong feelings do you experience when answering questions about your relationship with a Higher Power? _____

  _____

  _____

  _____

  _____

Allocate equal time for each family member. Please limit individual sharing to feelings and explanations of the written material. Allow time for contributions from family members after writing has been shared.

FAMILY GROUP CONTACT RECORD
WEEK 8

Date: _____ Person _____ Subject _____

Result of communication and action taken: _____

_____

_____

_____

Feelings experienced (love, anger, pain, support, acknowledgement): _____

_____

_____

_____

Date: _____ Person _____ Subject _____

Result of communication and action taken: _____

_____

_____

_____

Feelings experienced (love, anger, pain, support, acknowledgement): _____

_____

_____

_____

Summary of Week's events: _____

_____

_____

_____

_____

_____

_____

_____

_____

_____

_____

Week 9 Writing Exercise focuses on the *Higher Power Exercise.*

STEP THREE
PROCESSES AND QUESTIONS FOR WEEK 8 (Step 3 — Week 1)

Made a decision to turn our will and our lives over
to the care of God as we understood God.

FOOTPRINTS

One night a woman had a dream. She dreamed she was walking along the beach with her Higher Power. Across the sky flashed scenes from her life. For each scene, she noticed two sets of footprints in the sand; one belonged to her, and the other to her Higher Power. When the last scene of her life flashed before her, she looked back at the footprints in the sand. She noticed that many times along the path of her life there was only one set of footprints. She also noticed that it happened at the very lowest and saddest times in her life. This really bothered her and she questioned her Higher Power about it. "Lord, you said that once I decided to follow you, you'd walk with me all the way. But I have noticed that during the most troublesome times in my life, there is only one set of footprints. I don't understand why when I needed you most you would leave me." The Lord replied, "My precious, precious child, I love you and would never leave you. During your times of trial and suffering, when you see only one set of footprints, it was then that I carried you.

- How do you relate **Footprints** to Step Three? _____
_____
_____
_____
_____
_____
_____
_____

- What are the main areas in your life that need to be turned over to God? Explain. _____
_____
_____
_____
_____
_____
_____
_____
_____

Allocate equal time for each family member. Please limit individual sharing to feelings and expla-nations of the written material. Allow time for contributions from family members after writing has been shared.

FAMILY GROUP CONTACT RECORD
WEEK 9

Date: _____ Person _____ Subject _____

Result of communication and action taken: _____

_____

_____

_____

Feelings experienced (love, anger, pain, support, acknowledgement): _____

_____

_____

_____

Date: _____ Person _____ Subject _____

Result of communication and action taken: _____

_____

_____

_____

Feelings experienced (love, anger, pain, support, acknowledgement): _____

_____

_____

_____

Summary of Week's events: _____

_____

_____

_____

_____

_____

_____

_____

_____

_____

_____

_____

_____

STEP THREE
PROCESSES AND QUESTIONS FOR WEEK 9 (Step 3 — Week 2)

*Made a decision to turn our will and our lives over
to the care of God as we understood God.*

- The purpose of the **Higher Power Exercise** is to identify key role models in your life. How does the writing process assist you in discovering how your Higher Power has worked through others? _____
_____
_____
_____
_____
_____
_____

- Cite situations during the week in which you turned to your Higher Power for guidance. How did you feel when you let go? _____
_____
_____
_____
_____
_____
_____

- What are you willing to do to improve the contact you have with your family group outside this meeting? What feelings are you willing to express about your family group contact? _____
_____
_____
_____
_____
_____
_____

Allocate equal time for each family member. Please limit individual sharing to feelings and explanations of the written material. Allow time for contributions from family members after writing has been shared.

FAMILY GROUP CONTACT RECORD
WEEK 10

Date: _____ Person _____ Subject _____

Result of communication and action taken: _____

_____

_____

_____

Feelings experienced (love, anger, pain, support, acknowledgement): _____

_____

_____

_____

Date: _____ Person _____ Subject _____

Result of communication and action taken: _____

_____

_____

_____

Feelings experienced (love, anger, pain, support, acknowledgement): _____

_____

_____

_____

Summary of Week's events: _____

_____

_____

_____

_____

_____

_____

_____

_____

_____

_____

Week 11 Writing Exercise focuses on the *Resentment* and *Fear Exercises*.

STEP FOUR
PROCESSES AND QUESTIONS FOR WEEK 10 (Step 4—Week 1)

Made a searching and fearless moral inventory of ourselves.

• In what areas of your life are you aware that you are using denial or rationalization (Refer to page 28)? How do you feel about your behavior? _____

_____

_____

_____

_____

_____

_____

• What kind of support do you want from your family group to help you complete Step Four (e.g., telephone support, meeting outside of regular meetings)? Please ask for what you want. People can't read your mind. _____

_____

_____

_____

_____

_____

• Respond to this statement: "Certain behaviors and personality traits we learned in childhood were normal (not sick) reactions to the conditions from which we came. These traits now cause inappropriate choices. The Steps are a way to help redefine how we choose." __

_____

_____

_____

_____

_____

Allocate equal time for each family member. Please limit individual sharing to feelings and explanations of the written material. Allow time for contributions from family members after writing has been shared.

FAMILY GROUP CONTACT RECORD
WEEK 11

Date: _____ Person _____ Subject _____

Result of communication and action taken: _____

_____

_____

_____

Feelings experienced (love, anger, pain, support, acknowledgement): _____

_____

_____

_____

Date: _____ Person _____ Subject _____

Result of communication and action taken: _____

_____

_____

_____

Feelings experienced (love, anger, pain, support, acknowledgement): _____

_____

_____

_____

Summary of Week's events: _____

_____

_____

_____

_____

_____

_____

_____

_____

_____

_____

_____

STEP FOUR
PROCESSES AND QUESTIONS FOR WEEK 11 (Step 4—Week 2)

Made a searching and fearless moral inventory of ourselves.

● What feelings surface when you read the following: "Working the Steps enables us to make healthier choices. This makes a difference in our ability to stop behaving inappropriately." _____

_____

_____

_____

_____

_____

_____

● Describe your main resentment and your main fear. What do you believe to be the underlying cause? Refer to the **Resentment** and **Fear Exercises.** _____

_____

_____

_____

_____

_____

_____

● In what way do you feel your relationship with your Higher Power is supporting you as you write your Fourth Step Inventory? _____

_____

_____

_____

_____

_____

Allocate equal time for each family member. Please limit individual sharing to feelings and explanations of the written material. Allow time for contributions from family members after writing has been shared.

FAMILY GROUP CONTACT RECORD
WEEK 12

Date: _____ Person _____ Subject _____

Result of communication and action taken: _____

_____

_____

_____

Feelings experienced (love, anger, pain, support, acknowledgement): _____

_____

_____

_____

Date: _____ Person _____ Subject _____

Result of communication and action taken: _____

_____

_____

_____

Feelings experienced (love, anger, pain, support, acknowledgement): _____

_____

_____

_____

Summary of Week's events: _____

_____

_____

_____

_____

_____

_____

_____

_____

_____

_____

_____

_____

STEP FOUR
PROCESSES AND QUESTIONS FOR WEEK 12 (Step 4—Week 3)

Made a searching and fearless moral inventory of ourselves.

Through your family group, you have a chance to test new behavior (e.g. trusting, honestly sharing feelings, telling the truth). Tonight's exercise is intended to identify and acknowledge strengths and positive qualities you have experienced in your family group members and in yourself. For each member of your family group, write in the space below the strengths or positive qualities you see in them. Do the same for yourself. In the space you use for yourself, write down the qualities your family group identifies for you.

- Strengths and positive qualities I experience in my family group:

  Member   Strengths   Positive Qualities

  _____

  _____

  _____

  _____

  _____

  _____

- Strengths and positive qualities I see in myself:

  Strengths: _____

  _____

  _____

  Positive qualities:_____

  _____

  _____

- Strengths and positive qualities others see in me (complete this section as your family group shares with you the qualities they experience in you):

  Strengths: _____

  _____

  _____

  Positive Qualities: _____

  _____

  _____

Allocate equal time for each family member. Please limit individual sharing to feelings and explanations of the written material. Allow time for contributions from family members after writing has been shared.

FAMILY GROUP CONTACT RECORD
WEEK 13

Date: _____ Person _____ Subject _____

Result of communication and action taken: _____

_____

_____

_____

Feelings experienced (love, anger, pain, support, acknowledgement): _____

_____

_____

_____

Date: _____ Person _____ Subject _____

Result of communication and action taken: _____

_____

_____

_____

Feelings experienced (love, anger, pain, support, acknowledgement): _____

_____

_____

_____

Summary of Week's events: _____

_____

_____

_____

_____

_____

_____

_____

_____

_____

_____

Week 14 Writing Exercise focuses on *Guidelines for Preparing Your Fifth Step*.

STEP FIVE
PROCESSES AND QUESTIONS FOR WEEK 13 (Step 5—Week 1)

Admitted to God, to ourselves, and to another human
being the exact nature of our wrongs.

- What is your reaction to the following statement. "This is not the only time you will do the Fifth Step. It begins the process of becoming aware of your humanness." _____

_____

_____

_____

_____

_____

- How do you feel about the members of your family group? _____

_____

_____

_____

_____

_____

- What have you been unwilling to ask for from your family group? What are you willing to ask for now? _____

_____

_____

_____

_____

_____

- What have you been unwilling to give to your family group? What are you now willing to give or commit to your family group? _____

_____

_____

_____

_____

_____

Allocate equal time for each family member. Please limit individual sharing to feelings and explanations of the written material. Allow time for contributions from family members after writing has been shared.

The 12 Steps—A Way Out

FAMILY GROUP CONTACT RECORD
WEEK 14

Date: _____ Person _____ Subject _____
Result of communication and action taken: _____
_____
_____
_____

Feelings experienced (love, anger, pain, support, acknowledgement): _____
_____
_____
_____

Date: _____ Person _____ Subject _____
Result of communication and action taken: _____
_____
_____
_____

Feelings experienced (love, anger, pain, support, acknowledgement): _____
_____
_____
_____

Summary of Week's events: _____
_____
_____
_____
_____
_____
_____
_____
_____
_____
_____
_____
_____

STEP FIVE
PROCESSES AND QUESTIONS FOR WEEK 14 (Step 5—Week 2)

Admitted to God, to ourselves, and to another human
being the exact nature of our wrongs.

● Review the **Guidelines For Preparing Your Fifth Step.** Describe how you plan to complete your Fifth Step. _____

_____

_____

_____

_____

_____

_____

_____

● What are you now willing to share about your inventory? Select a behavior that has been a problem, but you now see positive change and recovery taking place. _____

_____

_____

_____

_____

_____

_____

_____

_____

Special Note:
During your family group sharing experience, separate into pairs and share some part of your Fifth Step with your partner. This exercise will help you complete your Fifth Step with another person. As part of tonight's sharing, discuss any feelings you experienced during this interaction.

Allocate equal time for each family member. Please limit individual sharing to feelings and explanations of the written material. Allow time for contributions from family members after writing has been shared.

FAMILY GROUP CONTACT RECORD
WEEK 15

Date: _____ Person _____ Subject _____

Result of communication and action taken: _____

_____

_____

_____

_____

Feelings experienced (love, anger, pain, support, acknowledgement): _____

_____

_____

_____

Date: _____ Person _____ Subject _____

Result of communication and action taken: _____

_____

_____

_____

_____

Feelings experienced (love, anger, pain, support, acknowledgement): _____

_____

_____

_____

Summary of Week's events: _____

_____

_____

_____

_____

_____

_____

_____

_____

_____

_____

_____

_____

WEEK 15

SUGGESTIONS RELATIVE TO A STEP STUDY GROUP BREAK

At this point in the Step-Study process, it has proven helpful to use one of the meetings following Step Five to plan a break from the regular Step-Study routine. Having spent five or more weeks on Steps Four and Five, participants are oftentimes overwhelmed by their experiences. Some of them are behind in their writing and need time to catch up. This break is an opportunity for all the family groups to engage in an activity that is relaxing and allows time to socialize outside the regular Step-Study meeting.

Some suggestions are:

- Plan an evening out—dinner in a restaurant with a relaxing atmosphere or one with a "childlike," playful environment.

- Plan a potluck dinner (depending upon the time of year) that can be held outdoors in a restful, relaxed location.

- Plan a progressive dinner party; have different courses assigned to each "family group."

- Use the meeting time to play games (e.g. children's games, charades, non-competitive games).

- Use the meeting time to go to a movie, or rent a movie and have a potluck dinner at the meeting place.

- Spend the evening at an amusement park, have a cookout at the beach or park or go to a video game facility.

- Plan a birthday party for the "kids" who missed out when growing up.

FAMILY GROUP CONTACT RECORD
WEEK 16

Date: _____ Person _____ Subject _____

Result of communication and action taken: _____

_____

_____

_____

Feelings experienced (love, anger, pain, support, acknowledgement): _____

_____

_____

_____

Date: _____ Person _____ Subject _____

Result of communication and action taken: _____

_____

_____

_____

Feelings experienced (love, anger, pain, support, acknowledgement): _____

_____

_____

_____

Summary of Week's events: _____

_____

_____

_____

_____

_____

_____

_____

_____

_____

_____

STEP SIX
PROCESSES AND QUESTIONS FOR WEEK 16 (Step 6 — Week 1)

Were entirely ready to work in partnership with God
to remove our ineffective behavior.

BROKEN DREAMS

As children bring their broken toys
with tears for us to mend,
I brought my broken dreams to God
because He was my friend.
But then, instead of leaving Him
in peace to work alone,
I hung around and tried to help
with ways that were my own.
At last, I snatched them back and cried,
"How can you be so slow?"
"My child," God said,
"What could I do?
You never did let go."

Author unknown

- How does **Broken Dreams** remind you of your unwillingness to "let go?" _____

_____

_____

_____

_____

_____

_____

- Identify behavior changes that you attribute to "being entirely ready" to work in partnership with God to remove your ineffective behavior? _____

_____

_____

_____

_____

_____

_____

Allocate equal time for each family member. Please limit individual sharing to feelings and explanations of the written material. Allow time for contributions from family members after writing has been shared.

FAMILY GROUP CONTACT RECORD
WEEK 17

Date: _____ Person _____ Subject _____

Result of communication and action taken: _____

_____

_____

_____

Feelings experienced (love, anger, pain, support, acknowledgement): _____

_____

_____

_____

Date: _____ Person _____ Subject _____

Result of communication and action taken: _____

_____

_____

_____

Feelings experienced (love, anger, pain, support, acknowledgement): _____

_____

_____

_____

Summary of Week's events: _____

_____

_____

_____

_____

_____

_____

_____

_____

_____

_____

_____

STEP SEVEN
PROCESSES AND QUESTIONS FOR WEEK 17 (Step 7—Week 1)

Humbly asked God to help us remove our shortcomings.

PARADOXES OF PRAYER

I asked God for strength, that I might achieve
 I was made weak, that I might learn humbly to obey...
I asked for health, that I might do greater things
 I was given infirmity, that I might do better things...
I asked for riches, that I might be happy
 I was given poverty, that I might be wise...
I asked for power, that I might have the praise of men
 I was given weakness, that I might feel the need of God...
I asked for all things, that I might enjoy life
 I was given life, that I might enjoy all things...
I got nothing that I asked for—but everything I had hoped for
 Almost despite myself, my unspoken prayers were answered
I am among all, most richly blessed!

©Universal Press Syndicate

● How does **Paradoxes of Prayer** reflect your experiences with prayer? _____

_____

_____

_____

_____

_____

_____

● How has your Higher Power provided what you needed, but not necessarily what you

wanted? _____

_____

_____

_____

_____

_____

_____

Allocate equal time for each family member. Please limit individual sharing to feelings and explanations of the written material. Allow time for contributions from family members after writing has been shared.

FAMILY GROUP CONTACT RECORD
WEEK 18

Date: _____ Person _____ Subject _____

Result of communication and action taken: _____

_____

_____

_____

Feelings experienced (love, anger, pain, support, acknowledgement): _____

_____

_____

_____

Date: _____ Person _____ Subject _____

Result of communication and action taken: _____

_____

_____

_____

Feelings experienced (love, anger, pain, support, acknowledgement): _____

_____

_____

_____

Summary of Week's events: _____

_____

_____

_____

_____

_____

_____

_____

_____

_____

_____

STEP EIGHT
PROCESSES AND QUESTIONS FOR WEEK 18 (Step 8—Week 1)

*Made a list of all persons we had harmed, and
became willing to make amends to them all.*

- Describe a person to whom you have caused harm (e.g., Mary Ann, wife; ABC, Inc., employer; etc.). _____
  _____
  _____
  _____

- What behavior created the error (e.g., angry with her preoccupation with neighborhood gossip; used expense account for personal entertainment)? _____
  _____
  _____
  _____

- What was the effect on others (e.g., she appears resentful and is distant; expense was $45, and boss does not know)? _____
  _____
  _____
  _____

- What was the effect on you (e.g., guilt and shame for treating her so harshly; guilt and fear that I'll be found out)? _____
  _____
  _____
  _____
  _____

- Why and how do you see yourself as an important name on your amends list? _____
  _____
  _____
  _____
  _____

*Allocate equal time for each family member. Please limit individual sharing to feelings and expla-
nations of the written material. Allow time for contributions from family members after writing
has been shared.*

FAMILY GROUP CONTACT RECORD
WEEK 19

Date: _____ Person _____ Subject _____

Result of communication and action taken: _____

_____

_____

_____

Feelings experienced (love, anger, pain, support, acknowledgement): _____

_____

_____

_____

Date: _____ Person _____ Subject _____

Result of communication and action taken: _____

_____

_____

_____

Feelings experienced (love, anger, pain, support, acknowledgement): _____

_____

_____

_____

Summary of Week's events: _____

_____

_____

_____

_____

_____

_____

_____

_____

_____

_____

Week 20 Writing Exercise focuses on the *Amends to Others Exercise*.

STEP EIGHT
PROCESSES AND QUESTIONS FOR WEEK 19 (Step 8 — Week 2)

*Made a list of all persons we had harmed, and
became willing to make amends to them all.*

The following are three of the fifteen **"Traits of a Healthy Family,"** as described by Dolores Curran in her book under the same title.

Communication Trait #1: The "healthy" family communicates and listens.

Affirming and Supporting Trait #2: The "healthy" family affirms and supports one another.

Getting Help Trait #15: The "healthy" family admits to, and seeks help with, problems.

- What contact did you make with your Step Study family last week as part of being supported in making your amends list? Describe your experience of the communication. __

_____

_____

_____

_____

_____

- Describe your feelings about the openness in communication within your family group. __

_____

_____

_____

_____

_____

- What difficulties are you having in making your amends list? _____

_____

_____

_____

_____

_____

Allocate equal time for each family member. Please limit individual sharing to feelings and explanations of the written material. Allow time for contributions from family members after writing has been shared.

FAMILY GROUP CONTACT RECORD
WEEK 20

Date: _____ Person _____ Subject _____

Result of communication and action taken: _____

_____

_____

_____

Feelings experienced (love, anger, pain, support, acknowledgement): _____

_____

_____

_____

Date: _____ Person _____ Subject _____

Result of communication and action taken: _____

_____

_____

_____

Feelings experienced (love, anger, pain, support, acknowledgement): _____

_____

_____

_____

Summary of Week's events: _____

_____

_____

_____

_____

_____

_____

_____

_____

_____

_____

_____

Week 21 Writing Exercise focuses on the *Amends to Self Exercise*.

STEP NINE
PROCESSES AND QUESTIONS FOR WEEK 20 (Step 9—Week 1)

Made direct amends to such people wherever possible,
except when to do so would injure them or others.

- Select a person to whom an amend is necessary. List the ways in which you would communicate the amend (see **Amends to Others Exercise**). _____

  _____

  _____

  _____

  _____

  _____

  _____

  _____

- Identify the feelings you have as you think about making an amend to them. In what way do you feel powerless over these emotions? _____

  _____

  _____

  _____

  _____

  _____

  _____

  _____

  _____

  _____

Special Note:
During your family group sharing, separate into pairs and practice making the above amend with your partner. Pretend that your partner is the person to whom the amend is to be made. As part of tonight's sharing, discuss your experience of this interaction.

Allocate equal time for each family member. Please limit individual sharing to feelings and explanations of the written material. Allow time for contributions from family members after writing has been shared.

FAMILY GROUP CONTACT RECORD
WEEK 21

Date: _____ Person _____ Subject _____

Result of communication and action taken: _____

_____

_____

_____

Feelings experienced (love, anger, pain, support, acknowledgement): _____

_____

_____

_____

Date: _____ Person _____ Subject _____

Result of communication and action taken: _____

_____

_____

_____

Feelings experienced (love, anger, pain, support, acknowledgement): _____

_____

_____

_____

Summary of Week's events: _____

_____

_____

_____

_____

_____

_____

_____

_____

_____

_____

_____

_____

Week 22 Writing Exercise focuses on the *Daily Inventory Log*.

STEP NINE
PROCESSES AND QUESTIONS FOR WEEK 21 (Step 9—Week 2)

*Made direct amends to such people wherever possible,
except when to do so would injure them or others.*

● List some highlights of the amends letter to yourself (see **Amends to Self Exercise**). ___

_____

_____

_____

_____

_____

_____

_____

_____

● What part of your amends is directed to your inner child, who still fears abandonment
or rejection? How can you take better care of your inner child? _____

_____

_____

_____

_____

_____

_____

_____

_____

_____

_____

_____

_____

Special Note:
During your family group sharing, separate into pairs and practice making the above amend
with your partner. Pretend that your partner is you. As part of tonight's sharing, discuss your
experience of this situation.

*Allocate equal time for each family member. Please limit individual sharing to feelings and expla-
nations of the written material. Allow time for contributions from family members after writing
has been shared.*

FAMILY GROUP CONTACT RECORD
WEEK 22

Date: _____ Person _____ Subject _____

Result of communication and action taken: _____

_____

_____

_____

Feelings experienced (love, anger, pain, support, acknowledgement): _____

_____

_____

_____

Date: _____ Person _____ Subject _____

Result of communication and action taken: _____

_____

_____

_____

Feelings experienced (love, anger, pain, support, acknowledgement): _____

_____

_____

_____

Summary of Week's events: _____

_____

_____

_____

_____

_____

_____

_____

_____

_____

_____

_____

_____

STEP TEN
PROCESSES AND QUESTIONS FOR WEEK 22 (Step 10—Week 1)

Continued to take personal inventory and, when we
were wrong, promptly admitted it.

● Review your actions of last week as recorded on your **Daily Inventory Log.** In what area did you function well? In what area did you function poorly? _____

_____

_____

_____

_____

_____

_____

● List ways in which you sensed your Higher Power's presence as you dealt with a challenging situation. _____

_____

_____

_____

_____

_____

_____

● Describe an experience of negative behavior, during which you promptly admitted your error. How did you feel about this? _____

_____

_____

_____

_____

_____

_____

Allocate equal time for each family member. Please limit individual sharing to feelings and explanations of the written material. Allow time for contributions from family members after writing has been shared.

FAMILY GROUP CONTACT RECORD
WEEK 23

Date: _____ Person _____ Subject _____
Result of communication and action taken: _____
_____
_____
_____

Feelings experienced (love, anger, pain, support, acknowledgement): _____
_____
_____
_____

Date: _____ Person _____ Subject _____
Result of communication and action taken: _____
_____
_____
_____

Feelings experienced (love, anger, pain, support, acknowledgement): _____
_____
_____
_____

Summary of Week's events: _____
_____
_____
_____
_____
_____
_____
_____
_____
_____
_____
_____
_____

STEP TEN
PROCESSES AND QUESTIONS FOR WEEK 23 (Step 10—Week 2)

Continued to take personal inventory and, when we
were wrong, promptly admitted it.

● Review today's thoughts, words and actions. Describe how you experienced the following feelings and behaviors.

Selfishness: _____

_____

_____

Dishonesty: _____

_____

_____

Anger: _____

_____

_____

Fear: _____

_____

_____

● Review today's thoughts, words and actions. Describe how you experienced the following feelings and behaviors.

Generosity: _____

_____

_____

Honesty: _____

_____

_____

Calm: _____

_____

_____

Courage: _____

_____

_____

Allocate equal time for each family member. Please limit individual sharing to feelings and explanations of the written material. Allow time for contributions from family members after writing has been shared.

FAMILY GROUP CONTACT RECORD
WEEK 24

Date: _____ Person _____ Subject _____

Result of communication and action taken: _____

_____

_____

_____

Feelings experienced (love, anger, pain, support, acknowledgement): _____

_____

_____

_____

Date: _____ Person _____ Subject _____

Result of communication and action taken: _____

_____

_____

_____

Feelings experienced (love, anger, pain, support, acknowledgement): _____

_____

_____

_____

Summary of Week's events: _____

_____

_____

_____

_____

_____

_____

_____

_____

_____

_____

_____

STEP ELEVEN
PROCESSES AND QUESTIONS FOR WEEK 24 (Step 11—Week 1)

Sought through prayer and meditation to improve our conscious contact
with God as we understood God, praying only for knowledge of
God's will for us and for the power to carry that out.

- What thoughts persist that cause you to remain focused on "your will," even while praying for God's guidance? _____

  _____

  _____

  _____

  _____

  _____

  _____

- What methods of prayer and meditation have you found most useful? _____

  _____

  _____

  _____

  _____

  _____

  _____

- In what way has your family group been an instrument of your Higher Power? _____

  _____

  _____

  _____

  _____

  _____

  _____

Allocate equal time for each family member. Please limit individual sharing to feelings and explanations of the written material. Allow time for contributions from family members after writing has been shared.

FAMILY GROUP CONTACT RECORD
WEEK 25

Date: _____ Person _____ Subject _____

Result of communication and action taken: _____

_____

_____

_____

Feelings experienced (love, anger, pain, support, acknowledgement): _____

_____

_____

_____

Date: _____ Person _____ Subject _____

Result of communication and action taken: _____

_____

_____

_____

Feelings experienced (love, anger, pain, support, acknowledgement): _____

_____

_____

_____

Summary of Week's events: _____

_____

_____

_____

_____

_____

_____

_____

_____

_____

_____

_____

Week 26 Writing Exercise focuses on the *Twelve Step Exercise*.

STEP ELEVEN
PROCESSES AND QUESTIONS FOR WEEK 25 (Step 11—Week 2)

Sought through prayer and meditation to improve our conscious contact
with God as we understood God, praying only for knowledge of
God's will for us and for the power to carry that out.

PRAYER OF SAINT FRANCIS OF ASSISI

Lord, make me an instrument of Your peace!
Where there is hatred—let me sow love
Where there is injury—pardon
Where there is doubt—faith
Where there is despair—hope
Where there is darkness—light
Where there is sadness—joy
O Divine Master, grant that I may not so much seek
To be consoled—as to console
To be loved—as to love
for
It is in giving—that we receive
It is in pardoning—that we are pardoned
It is in dying—that we are born to eternal life.
Amen.

- How does the **Prayer of Saint Francis of Assisi** illustrate some experience you have had when seeking to do God's will? _____

_____

_____

_____

_____

_____

- Cite an example of your praying only for knowledge of God's will and for the power to carry it out. What was the outcome? _____

_____

_____

_____

_____

_____

Allocate equal time for each family member. Please limit individual sharing to feelings and explanations of the written material. Allow time for contributions from family members after writing has been shared.

FAMILY GROUP CONTACT RECORD
WEEK 26

Date: _____ Person _____ Subject _____

Result of communication and action taken: _____

_____

_____

_____

Feelings experienced (love, anger, pain, support, acknowledgement): _____

_____

_____

_____

Date: _____ Person _____ Subject _____

Result of communication and action taken: _____

_____

_____

_____

Feelings experienced (love, anger, pain, support, acknowledgement): _____

_____

_____

_____

Summary of Week's events: _____

_____

_____

_____

_____

_____

_____

_____

_____

_____

_____

_____

STEP TWELVE
PROCESSES AND QUESTIONS FOR WEEK 26 (Step 12—Week 1)

Having had a spiritual awakening as the result
of these steps, we tried to carry this message to others,
and to practice these principles in all our affairs.

● What do you see as the ongoing value of applying the Twelve Steps on a daily basis? ___

_____

_____

_____

_____

_____

_____

● In what way did the **Twelve Step Exercise** empower you to handle a life situation more effectively? What did you experience in the way of an unexpected solution? _____

_____

_____

_____

_____

_____

_____

● Describe a recent situation in which you shared the message of the Twelve Steps with someone. _____

_____

_____

_____

_____

_____

_____

Allocate equal time for each family member. Please limit individual sharing to feelings and explanations of the written material. Allow time for contributions from family members after writing has been shared.

FAMILY GROUP CONTACT RECORD
WEEK 27

Date: _____ Person _____ Subject _____

Result of communication and action taken: _____

_____

_____

_____

Feelings experienced (love, anger, pain, support, acknowledgement): _____

_____

_____

_____

Date: _____ Person _____ Subject _____

Result of communication and action taken: _____

_____

_____

_____

Feelings experienced (love, anger, pain, support, acknowledgement): _____

_____

_____

_____

Summary of Week's events: _____

_____

_____

_____

_____

_____

_____

_____

_____

_____

_____

_____

STEP TWELVE
PROCESSES AND QUESTIONS FOR WEEK 27 (Step 12—Week 2)

Having had a spiritual awakening as the result
of these steps, we tried to carry this message to others,
and to practice these principles in all our affairs.

This is the final Step Study writing exercise. It is an opportunity for you to acknowledge yourself for having the courage to stay and work with other committed people who are seeking a healthier way of life.

Complete the following statements as you now view your life:

- When I was a child, I_____

  _____

- As I grew into adulthood, I_____

  _____

- When I became aware of my behavior, I_____

  _____

- Having completed the Step Study, I_____

  _____

As we may view our lives right now, we are the pens through which the ink of our Higher Power flows to write the story of our life. Our Step work and family group have contributed to our deeper contact with God. Sharing each other's experiences, strengths and hopes has enabled us to expand our faith in our Higher Power and experience unconditional love.

What do you want to say to your family members or to the other individuals of the Step Study relative to:

- Your spiritual awakening?:_____

  _____

  _____

- Your gratitude for their coaching you?:_____

  _____

  _____

- Your commitment to continue working the Steps?:_____

  _____

  _____

Allocate equal time for each family member. Please limit individual sharing to feelings and expla-
nations of the written material. Allow time for contributions from family members after writing
has been shared.

FAMILY GROUP CONTACT RECORD
WEEK 28

Date: _____ Person _____ Subject _____

Result of communication and action taken: _____

_____

_____

_____

Feelings experienced (love, anger, pain, support, acknowledgement): _____

_____

_____

_____

Date: _____ Person _____ Subject _____

Result of communication and action taken: _____

_____

_____

_____

Feelings experienced (love, anger, pain, support, acknowledgement): _____

_____

_____

_____

Summary of Week's events: _____

_____

_____

_____

_____

_____

_____

_____

_____

_____

_____

_____

CLOSING MEETING
PROCESSES AND QUESTIONS FOR WEEK 28

The facilitator(s) for this meeting can use the same time sequence as that for family group writing and sharing, ending with all the family groups joining together.

This meeting will complete the cycle of work you have done with your family group and the Twelve Steps.

Each person has the opportunity to gently say goodbye with joy, acknowledgement and love. It is most useful if everyone spends the writing time reflecting and writing on the following questions. Saying "thank you" individually and specifically is not necessary. Feelings of gratitude can be communicated within the question responses.

● I want to complete this experience by acknowledging that it has had the following meaning for me: _____

_____

_____

_____

_____

● As part of saying goodbye, I want to acknowledge how I feel about this ending. Feel free to express your present emotional state—it is a healthy part of accepting this change (e.g., loss sadness, fear, joy, anticipation, gratefulness). _____

_____

_____

_____

GROUP CLOSING

This closing affirmation is intended to initiate the large group closing. Further statements can be offered by each participant.

> "I dedicate myself to the love and care of my Higher Power. All healing work is the result of my partnership with my Higher Power. I am committed to surrendering all concerns, from the largest to the smallest, to my Higher Power. I accept that my self-will no longer needs to control my beliefs, thoughts or actions. Each day, I give thanks for the part of me that is being healed. I cooperate with this healing by agreeing to face any discomfort, knowing my Higher Power is there. I know that my healing is a source of joy and serenity to me. I am ever-open for the opportunity to spread the truth and the joy of my recovery, one day at a time."

Allocate equal time for each family member. Please limit individual sharing to feelings and explanations of the written material. Allow time for contributions from family members after writing has been shared.

Notes: _____

_____

_____

_____

_____

_____

_____

_____

_____

_____

_____

_____

_____

_____

_____

_____

_____

_____

_____

_____

_____

_____

_____

_____

_____

_____

_____

_____

_____

_____

_____

APPENDIX FOUR

SUGGESTED FORMAT FOR AN ONGOING FAMILY GROUP STEP STUDY

At the completion of the Step Study Writing Workshop, some group members may want to meet occasionally for support and renewal. It is possible to design a meeting that will fit the time and needs of the individuals involved. Any or all of the following can be utilized in the meeting format.

- **Opening prayer or meditation.**
- **Reading of** *Milestones in Recovery, The Twelve Steps for Adult Children* **or other recovery related material.**
- **Reflection and writing on the selected material.**
- **Personal sharing of experiences, problems or areas of concern.**
- **Restatement of mutual commitment to recovery.**
- **Closing prayers, affirmations or meditation.**

Opening Prayer or Meditation

"We give thanks to our Higher Power for this day, and for the gift of being together. We claim our Higher Power's presence within each of us, as we work to be healed and to find God's will for our lives. We ask for strength to care for ourselves and each other.

We come here to this place to be together as children of God, secure in the knowledge that God is enfolding us in love and peace—as we seek to help each other."

Reading of The Twelve Steps for Adult Children, Milestones In Recovery, etc.

Choose one or more of the Steps or Milestones for each meeting. See Appendix Two. Ask someone to read the selected material.

Reflection and Writing on the Selected Material

Reflection on selected material, after a period of writing, followed by each individual sharing how their recovery program is working. For example:

- *This (Step or Milestone) has meaning for me and relates to my life because…*
- *The guidance in this (Step or Milestone) can assist my recovery because…*
- *I desire to deepen my understanding of this (Step or Milestone)…*

Personal Sharing

Group members can contribute any recent experience of recovery or their writing responses. If you feel a need to respond to a group member and want to say something supportive, review the **Personal Statements and Affirmations** on the next page.

Restatement of Mutual Commitment to Recovery

We trust that God is with us as we work to strengthen our resolve to be healed to wholeness. God's presence keeps our hearts and minds directed toward our recovery. We acknowledge and avow our support for each other.

Closing Prayers, Affirmations or Meditations

We promise to keep whatever is shared within the confines of the group, in order to provide the atmosphere of safety necessary for openness.

PERSONAL STATEMENTS AND AFFIRMATIONS

The following statements and affirmations can be made to a group member, either aloud or silently, as an expression of support.

Affirmation

Nothing you have done or will do can separate you from your Higher Power or from my loving concern. I may not agree with your actions, but I will love you as a person and do all I can to hold you in thoughts of affirming love.

Prayer

I promise to lovingly hold you in my thoughts, believing that my Higher Power wishes only good to come to you.

Openness

I promise to strive to become a more open person, disclosing my feelings, my struggles, my joys and my hurts as well as I am able. I will succeed only if I can trust you with my problems and my dreams. I extend my trust to you and affirm your worth to me as a person and as a partner in my recovery.

Confidentiality

I promise to keep whatever is shared within the confines of the group, in order to provide the atmosphere of safety necessary for openness.

Availability

Anything I have—time, energy, insight, etc.—is at your disposal, to the limit of my resources. As part of this availability, I pledge my time on a regular basis, whether in prayer or in an agreed-upon meeting.

Honesty

I agree to tell the truth, so far as I know it, even if it means risking pain for either of us. I will trust our relationship enough to take that risk, realizing that it is in speaking the truth in love that we will find fulfillment in all things. I will try to express this honesty in a sensitive and loving manner.

Sensitivity

My desire is to be known and understood by you. I commit to understanding you and your needs to the best of my ability.

Accountability

I will seek the loving sharing of my supportive friends, so that I might give more of myself. I understand that I am accountable for the choices I make in my life.

APPENDIX FIVE

FAMILY GROUP TELEPHONE LIST

Name	Telephone No. (Work/Time)	Best Time To Call
1. _____	_____ (W) _____ (H)	_____ _____
2. _____	_____ (W) _____ (H)	_____ _____
3. _____	_____ (W) _____ (H)	_____ _____
4. _____	_____ (W) _____ (H)	_____ _____
5. _____	_____ (W) _____ (H)	_____ _____
6. _____	_____ (W) _____ (H)	_____ _____
7. _____	_____ (W) _____ (H)	_____ _____

TELEPHONE NUMBERS OF OTHER WORKSHOP PARTICIPANTS

1. _____	_____ (W) _____ (H)	_____ _____
2. _____	_____ (W) _____ (H)	_____ _____
3. _____	_____ (W) _____ (H)	_____ _____
4. _____	_____ (W) _____ (H)	_____ _____
5. _____	_____ (W) _____ (H)	_____ _____
6. _____	_____ (W) _____ (H)	_____ _____
7. _____	_____ (W) _____ (H)	_____ _____

APPENDIX SIX
SUGGESTED READING

Alcoholics Anonymous. **The Big Book.** New York, NY: Alcoholics Anonymous World Services, Inc.

Alcoholics Anonymous. **Twelve Steps—Twelve Traditions.** New York, NY: Alcoholics Anonymous World Services, Inc.

Beattie, Melody. **Codependent No More.** New York, NY: Harper and Row Publishers, Inc.

Black, Claudia. **It Will Never Happen To Me.** New York, NY: Ballantine Books.

Bradshaw, John. **Bradshaw on: The Family.** Deerfield Beach, FL: Health Communications, Inc.

Covington, Stephanie & Beckett, Liana. **Leaving The Enchanted Forest: The Path From Relationship Addiction To Intimacy.** New York, NY: Harper & Row.

Fishel, Ruth. **The Journey Within—A Spiritual Path To Recovery.** Deerfield Beach, FL: Health Communications, Inc.

Friel, John and Friel, Linda. **Adult Children—The Secrets of Dysfunctional Families.** Deerfield Beach, FL: Health Communications, Inc.

Friends in Recovery. **The 12 Steps for Adult Children.** San Diego, CA: Recovery Publications.

Friends in Recovery. **The Twelve Steps—A Spiritual Journey.** San Diego, CA: Recovery Publications.

Friends in Recovery. **The Twelve Steps for Christians.** San Diego, CA: Recovery Publications.

Kritsberg, Wayne. **The Adult Children of Alcoholics Syndrome.** Deerfield Beach, FL: Health Communications, Inc.

Larson, Earnie and Hegarty, Carol. **Days of Healing—Days of Joy.** New York, NY: Harper/Hazelden.

Lasater, Lane. **Recovery From Compulsive Behavior.** Deerfield Beach, FL: Health Communications, Inc.

Lerner, Rokelle. **Daily Affirmations—For Adult Children of Alcoholics.** Deerfield Beach, FL: Health Communications, Inc.

Pollard, Dr. John K., III. **Self Parenting: Your Complete Guide to Inner Conversations.** Malibu, CA: Generic Human Studies Publishing.

Smith, Ann W. **Grandchildren of Alcoholics—Another Generation of Codependency.** Deerfield Beach, FL: Health Communications, Inc.

Wegscheider-Cruse, Sharon. **Learning To Love Yourself.** Deerfield Beach, FL: Health Communications, Inc.

Whitfield, Charles. **Healing the Child Within.** Deerfield Beach, FL: Health Communications, Inc.

Woititz, Janet. **Adult Children of Alcoholics.** Deerfield Beach, FL: Health Communications, Inc.

Woititz, Janet G. **Struggle For Intimacy.** Deerfield Beach, FL: Health Communications, Inc.

ORDER FORM

CODE	TITLE	QTY	UNIT PRICE	TOTAL
4001	The Big Book, Alcoholics Anonymous	___	$ 6.00	___
4002	Twelve Steps—Twelve Traditions	___	$ 5.00	___
1016	Codependent No More	___	$ 8.95	___
1058	It Will Never Happen To Me	___	$ 3.95	___
2091	Bradshaw on: The Family	___	$ 9.95	___
2228	Leaving The Enchanted Forest: The Path From Relationship Addition To Intimacy	___	$10.95	___
4097	The Journey Within—A Spiritual Path To Recovery	___	$ 8.95	___
1085	Adult Children—The Secrets of Dysfunctional Families	___	$ 8.95	___
9901	The 12 Steps—A Way Out	___	$14.95	___
9902	The 12 Steps for Adult Children	___	$ 7.95	___
9903	The Twelve Steps—A Spiritual Journey	___	$14.95	___
9904	The Twelve Steps for Christians	___	$ 7.95	___
1038	The ACoA Syndrome	___	$ 7.95	___
3087	Days of Healing—Days of Joy	___	$ 6.95	___
2111	Recovery From Compulsive Behavior	___	$ 7.95	___
3024	Daily Affirmations—For Adult Children of Alcoholics	___	$ 6.95	___
6083	Self Parenting: Your Complete Guide to Inner Conversations	___	$ 9.95	___
2026	Grandchildren of Alcoholics/Another Generation of Codependency	___	$ 8.95	___
1027	Learning To Love Yourself	___	$ 7.95	___
1029	Healing the Child Within	___	$ 8.95	___
1034	Adult Children of Alcoholics	___	$ 6.95	___
1075	Struggle For Intimacy	___	$ 6.95	___

Sub-Total _____

*Sales Tax _____

**Shipping & Handling _____

TOTAL _____

Send this order form and a check or money order for the total to:

TOOLS FOR RECOVERY
1201 Knoxville Street
San Diego, CA 92110

To order by phone, please call
(619) 275-1350

Name: _____

Address: _____

City/State: _____

Zip: _____ Phone: (____) _____

*6% Sales Tax (CA Residents only)

**Shpg. & Hand. Min. Charge —	$3.00
Orders over $25.00 —	$5.00
Orders over $50.00 —	6% of Total

Visa and MasterCard Accepted

Bankcard # _____

Expiration Date _____

Signature _____

Allow 2-3 weeks for delivery — UPS